Amateurs without Borders

Amateurs without Borders

THE ASPIRATIONS AND LIMITS OF GLOBAL COMPASSION

Allison Schnable

UNIVERSITY OF CALIFORNIA PRESS

University of California Press
Oakland, California

© 2021 by Allison Schnable

Library of Congress Cataloging-in-Publication Data

Names: Schnable, Allison, 1981– author.
Title: Amateurs without borders : the aspirations and limits of global
    compassion / Allison Schnable.
Description: Oakland, California : University of California Press, [2021] |
    Includes bibliographical references and index.
Identifiers: LCCN 2020026932 (print) | LCCN 2020026933 (ebook) |
    ISBN 9780520300941 (cloth) | ISBN 9780520300958 (paperback) |
    ISBN 9780520972124 (epub)
Subjects: LCSH: Non-governmental organizations—History—20th
    century. | Non-governmental organizations—History—21st century.
Classification: LCC JZ4841 .S35 2021 (print) | LCC JZ4841 (ebook) |
    DDC 361.7/7—dc23
LC record available at https://lccn.loc.gov/2020026932
LC ebook record available at https://lccn.loc.gov/2020026933

29   28   27   26   25   24   23   22   21   20
10   9   8   7   6   5   4   3   2   1

Contents

Illustrations

Acknowledgments

This project had its beginnings in late-night conversations with fellow Peace Corps volunteers under the Senegalese moon. But it took shape thanks to the resources of an intellectual community that I acknowledge here with gratitude.

I am grateful to have received the Lake Institute Dissertation Fellowship and the Charlotte Newcombe Dissertation Fellowship, which provided ample funding and time to carry out this research as a PhD student. At Princeton University, the Sociology Department, Center for the Study of Religion, Center for Arts and Cultural Policy Studies, Fellowship of Woodrow Wilson Scholars, and Program on International and Regional Studies also funded my research and offered chances to present my work in progress; this book is stronger for it. Thanks also to the Faculty Writing Groups at Indiana University, led by Laura Plummer, for creating a congenial environment in which I could work on this manuscript.

The Center for the Study of Religion was my intellectual home at Princeton, and I thank Director Emeritus Robert Wuthnow, Associate Director Jenny Wiley Legath, and Center Manager Anita Kline for cultivating such a remarkable intellectual environment there. The smart and congenial fellows I encountered at CSR over seven years are too many to name, but I especially acknowledge Gill Frank, Erin Johnston, and Carol Ann MacGregor. LiErin Probasco, Steve Offutt, and Amy Reynolds were particularly helpful interlocutors on the questions of religion and development.

Thank you to Woody Powell, Rob Reich, Johanna Mair, and Paul Brest for invitations to the Stanford Center on Philanthropy and Civil Society Junior Scholars Forum in 2014 and 2019. The feedback at these workshops and the community of scholars you fostered there are unparalleled. I also thank Anke Schwittay and Anne-Meike Fechter for convening a workshop on citizen aid at the University of Sussex in 2018 and all of the attendees for a very fruitful exchange of ideas. I especially note Sara Kinsbergen, who has done leading work on similar organizations in the Netherlands and who has been very gracious in sharing her data, and Susan Appe, who has been a wonderful colleague in looking at capacity building for grassroots international NGOs. I am grateful to Ann Swidler and Judith Lasker for their thoughtful comments on this manuscript, and to Naomi Schneider and her crack team at University of California Press for shepherding the book into print.

This work was realized with the help of several top-shelf research assistants. Anna Graziano oversaw the collection of website addresses, Michael Franklin assisted with topic modeling, Colin Fisk assisted with graphs, and April Byrne and Janet Jock capably handled fact checking and a number of editorial tasks. Thank you to then fellow graduate students Manish Nag, who wrote a program to help me collect data from websites, and Beth Sully, who was my travel companion in East Africa.

I am deeply grateful for the guidance and generosity of Princeton University Sociology faculty, and particularly the members of my dissertation committee, each of whom has shaped me as a scholar and person: Robert Wuthnow, Miguel Centeno, Paul DiMaggio, and Stan Katz. I have been uncommonly lucky to work with you all.

The O'Neill School of Public and Environmental Affairs at Indiana University could not have been more generous or encouraging to a junior faculty member. I thank my faculty colleagues, graduate students, and the school's leadership past and present, particularly Kirsten Grønbjerg and Michael McGuire. I want to acknowledge with thanks Indiana University's efforts to help faculty balance their work and family commitments; in another time or place, I would have had to choose between this project and my family. The Lilly Family School of Philanthropy has also provided support and intellectual community for my work. Thanks to Tim Hallett and Fabio Rojas for their suggestions on the manuscript at key junctures, and to the rest of the Sociology Department at Indiana University for welcoming a redheaded stepchild into the department's community.

Perhaps the best thing about academic life is the opportunity to work with one's friends. Sofya Aptekar, Yael Berda, Jennifer Brass, Chris DeSante, Wes Longhofer, Rachel Sullivan Robinson, Rafael Treibich, and Cristobal Young have provided help when I asked for it and encouragement when I needed it; thank you, with love. I thank my family and especially my mother, June Youatt, whose example made all of this seem possible.

The leaders and volunteers of the organizations I write about here did me a great kindness in speaking frankly about their work and in many cases inviting me into their homes. Although I critique some of their ideas and efforts here, I hope I have lived up to my promise not to be glib. It's much easier to critique from the sidelines than to do the messy work of trying to translate compassion into real improvement in the lives of the poor. The volunteers I discuss here were doubly compassionate, first in their efforts abroad and second in making themselves vulnerable to the questions of an inquisitive stranger. These people have my respect and gratitude.

Introduction

The only ice-cream shop in Butare, Rwanda, is the offspring of a chance encounter at the Sundance Institute. The leader of a women's drumming group from East Africa fell into conversation with two restaurateurs from Brooklyn who had recently opened an ice-cream shop that was winning the hearts of New York's foodies. In the space of a few months, the plan emerged for Inzozi Nziza: an ice-cream parlor in a Rwandan university neighborhood, funded by the Brooklyn restaurateurs and staffed by the young women who played in the drumming group. The young women would receive training in English and business management, while the appeal of ice cream on hot East African afternoons would eventually make the project self-sustaining. The three partners hired a former Peace Corps volunteer to oversee the training and launch of the shop in Butare, and in January 2011 the new organization was registered with the IRS as Blue Marble Dreams. Suddenly the Brooklyn foodies were the heads of a nongovernmental organization (NGO).

Blue Marble Dreams is one of more than 10,000 new international aid organizations founded by Americans since 1990. Thanks to the world-shrinking power of globalization, Americans find themselves connected to distant communities in the poor regions of the world. Beneath the global exchanges of trade and the movements of a cosmopolitan elite, American citizens are more quietly forging global ties through immigration, tourism, volunteering, study, work, and adoption. These ties have made possible a new wave of grassroots development aid. In 1990, there were just over 1,000 international aid organizations registered with the US Internal Revenue Service. Over the years the numbers have grown, such that more than 1,300 *new* organizations were established in 2010 alone. By the end of 2015, a total of 13,030 aid organizations were active. They are now based in one out of every three US counties. These groups signal a transformation in the way Americans engage in global activism and charity.

Organizations focused on international issues are a small part of the US nonprofit sector, but they have been growing much more quickly than other types of nonprofits in the last three decades. The number of new international aid groups registering annually with the IRS quadrupled from 2000 to 2010, compared with only 19 percent growth for other 501(c)3s (see figure 1). Charitable giving echoes the story: Americans gave $23 billion to internationally focused organizations in 2017. Giving to such groups grew faster between 2010 and 2016 (roughly 8% per year) than giving to education, health, the arts, or religion.[1]

To make sense of this organizational expansion, we have to understand that most of the ten thousand new organizations resemble Blue Marble Dreams more than well-known international NGOs like CARE or World Vision. These new groups rely largely on volunteer labor and individual donations rather than contract revenue or foundation grants. IRS records show that the median organization has an annual budget of $25,000 or less, and three-quarters operate on $134,000 or less annually. Only the top

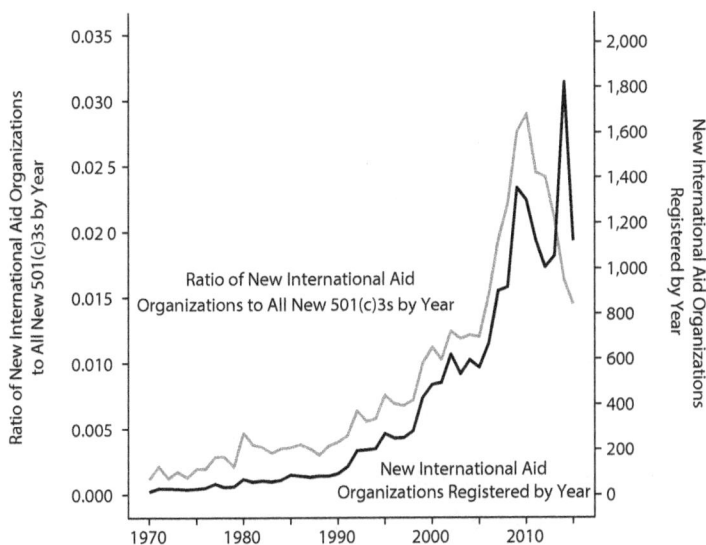

FIGURE 1. New international aid organizations registered annually with the IRS, 1970–2015. *Source:* National Center for Charitable Statistics Master File and IRS Business Master Files.

8 percent of US-registered international aid organizations draw annual revenue of $1 million or more.[2]

These groups are typically personal projects launched by Americans with a college degree but no professional experience in international development. Adoptive parents want to provide extra help to their child's native town; MBA students want to try out an idea for improving small-scale farming; an immigrant wants to set up a school in his home country; a pastor wants to dig wells in arid African villages. The people who initiate these projects are rarely development experts or seasoned activists. They are more likely teachers, accountants, or IT specialists who cut their teeth on church work or volunteer service. Work and leisure travel takes them to developing countries, where they forge relationships that inspire aid projects. But these American volunteers cultivate the projects while they remain embedded in their careers and communities in the United States, unlike full-time, trained aid workers whose orientation is to the professional field of development.[3] Because they are largely self-financed and separated from the professional development field, and because they emerge from personal relationships, these organizations reject expert prescriptions in favor of aid approaches that are more expressive and personal.

I refer to these new organizations as grassroots international nongovernmental organizations. The name acknowledges their similarity in purpose to well-known international nongovernmental organizations, or INGOs, while distinguishing their crucial differences in size, scale, geographic reach, budgets, and international visibility. The adjective *grassroots* signals these organizations' small scale and do-it-yourself flavor, and emphasizes that they typically work directly with recipients rather than transmitting aid through a long chain of organizations.[4] (For brevity's sake I will use the term *grassroots INGO* in this book. When discussing ideas or research projects that do not distinguish between local or international NGOs, I will simply refer to *NGOs*. I discuss these terms in greater detail in appendix 1 on my methodology.)

Fifty years ago, a few of these groups' intrepid founders would have set off as Peace Corps volunteers or missionaries, but most of them would have just sent checks to large NGOs. Why so many groups like Blue Marble Dreams now? The emergence of grassroots INGOs is part of the broader story of "the rise and rise" of NGOs as actors in international affairs. But NGOs' rise had been accompanied—inextricably, it seemed—by their professionalization. Like other nonprofit organizations, NGOs have increasingly become guided by manager-experts, making them look more like government agencies and corporations than fluid expressions of civic energy. NGO scholar-practitioners Shepard Forman and Abby Stoddard wrote of NGO work in 2002 that "the era of well-meaning amateurs has given way to an epistemic community of well-trained professionals."[5] So how do we get ice-cream shop owners starting an NGO with Rwandan musicians? How do we find a self-described Baptist "cowboy-pastor" at the head of an NGO that operates schools and clinics, and volunteers from Texas who describe their work in Bosnia as a "transatlantic barn-raising?" In short, globalization has transformed the way people can organize, and has put NGO work back in the hands of amateurs.

How Did We Get Here?

The "Rise and Rise" of NGOs . . .

Nongovernmental organizations have played a role in relief and development aid for at least seventy years. The first baby boom of American NGOs came in the wake of World War II, when the US government leaned on CARE, Lutheran World Relief, Catholic Relief Services, and their ilk to provide relief to a devastated Europe after the war.[6] With this task complete by the 1950s, these organizations turned toward Africa, Latin America, and Asia, and Northern governments began to distribute bilateral aid for development.

The US government became increasingly disgruntled with foreign aid in the 1970s. The Senate Foreign Operations Subcommittee, which held the foreign aid purse strings, expressed frustration at the lack of fruit borne by aid sent directly to governments of less-developed countries. The result was a plan in the 1973 Foreign

Assistance Act to channel more aid through nongovernmental organizations rather than through receiving-country governments.[7] The 1950s and '60s approach to development had centered on technical assistance and developing infrastructure. The idea was that in Asia, Latin America, and Africa, as in reconstructed Europe, (capitalist) industrial development would generate a rising tide that would lift all boats. The shift toward NGOs in the 1970s thus also entailed a switch in tactics toward meeting the basic needs of the poor for food, water, health, and education.

Two political developments in the 1980s catalyzed the growth of NGOs. The first was Reagan-Thatcherist politics, which whittled away at the role of the state in providing social services. Nongovernmental organizations were increasingly relied upon— by design or default—to carry out the tasks that until recently had fallen to government.[8] The second catalyst was the dissolution of the Soviet Union and the perceived role of civil society therein. Western leaders were encouraged by the success of the nascent civil society in Eastern Europe and eagerly donated millions of dollars in an attempt to establish the organizations they believed were crucial for stable democracy.[9] Donors' enthusiasm for civil society as a path to both democratization and development once again carried over from Europe to the global South. NGOs became an institution that both the political left and right could embrace. For the right, they were a means of keeping governments small; for the left, they were a political force that could challenge existing power relations.[10] NGOs also expanded their roles in response to humanitarian crises. Media coverage of the 1980s Ethiopian famines was a turning point, as the graphic images of children's suffering broadcast on the evening news brought public outcry and support for humanitarian action. Forman and Stoddard note the role relief organizations took on in civil wars and other unstable situations in subsequent years. They argue that citizens of wealthy countries had little taste for casualties in peacekeeping or humanitarian emergencies, and so giving aid via NGOs became the "weapon of first resort" in these situations.[11]

Huge sums of money now flow through nongovernmental organizations. In 2011, $19.3 billion in official development aid was budgeted to or through NGOs, or about 15 percent of all official aid from OECD countries.[12] For the United States, 23 percent of official aid went to NGOs. This excludes private charitable donations, which in 2010 totaled another $14 billion for US NGOs and in 2011 $32 billion for NGOs based in all OECD member countries.[13] In other words, nearly half of all public and private US dollars for relief and development now go to NGOs.

NGOs rose to prominence in no small part because of political opportunities. The governments of less-developed countries came to be seen as unsavory partners, state provision of social services fell out of favor as neoliberal politics ascended, and NGOs were envisioned as the catalyst for civil society and thus for democracy outside of the West. Yet NGOs have been able to exploit these opportunities because of their particular cultural status.[14] As Dorothea Hilhorst argues, the title "NGO" is a "claim-bearing label." NGOs are part of a lineage of charitable organizations in the Anglo world that goes back to the Elizabethan Statute of Charitable Uses. For more than four hundred years, groups that aid the needy and keep no profit have enjoyed special legal recognition and public legitimacy. When someone undertakes international development work under the aegis of an NGO, she benefits from that legacy; as Hilhorst points out: "The label has a moral component. Precisely because it is doing good, the organization can make a bid to access funding and public representation."[15] This moral legitimacy and favorable legal treatment have bolstered NGOs into the twenty-first century.

. . . And Their Professionalization

The story of the "rise and rise" of NGOs over the last four decades, as Edwards and Hulme characterize it, has involved the professionalization of NGOs.[16] Historical, theoretical, and empirical accounts have all described the increasing rationalization and professionalization of the nonprofit sector, of which NGOs are part.[17] Hwang and Powell carried out a major study in the San Francisco Bay area to learn about the operations of a random sample of nonprofit organizations. They found that the use of consultants, strategic planning, independent financial audits, and data for program evaluation—techniques ubiquitous in the for-profit (and in some cases the government) sector—had become common. These strategies were more likely to be used when the nonprofits were funded by foundations, had full-time staff, and had executives with professional degrees (particularly MBAs or other training in management). In other words, being a full-time, "professional" organization, rather than a part-time, volunteer-driven group, means relying on data and expert advice and using formal processes for planning and evaluating outcomes. Hwang and Powell saw professionalization infiltrating a range of social domains, including those that were once homely and intimate; even "the sage advice of grandmothers has been supplanted by a wide array of child development experts and agencies."[18]

Forman and Stoddard argued that this trend was a dominant force in the field of international NGOs and predicted a "homogenization" of NGOs driven both by professional norms and stiff competition among NGOs for external funds.[19] Their story is consistent with the trajectory of the major American NGOs that emerged during and just after the World Wars. A host of religious and ethnically oriented NGOs were founded during this period to provide relief, including the American Friends Service Committee, the Jewish Joint Distribution Committee, Church World Service, Lutheran World Relief, CARE, and Catholic Relief Services. World Vision was founded in 1950 to provide direct aid to missionaries and orphans in Asia. All of these organizations remain major providers of relief or development services today, with Catholic Relief Services and World Vision among the top contractors for the US Agency for International Development (USAID), wielding a combined $300 million in annual government funding.[20]

One telling fact of professionalization is that religious organizations create ways to compartmentalize their religious expression in order to maintain legitimacy in the field of aid organizations. Agensky describes both the structural constraints (i.e., donors' rules) and normalizing forces (i.e., professional practices) that integrate large religious NGOs into the mainstream aid field. He finds that evangelical Christian aid workers "described themselves as being professional relief workers first." Listening to aid workers' complaints about religiously motivated "amateurs" working in the same region, Agensky notes the "tension" that exists "between professional and informal organisations that exemplify different modes of humanitarian imaginaries. Ideologically driven groups, as well as inexperienced 'do gooders' and 'well wishers'. . . pose a large problem for all professional faith-based relief workers."[21]

The NGO employees shared religious commitments with the "ideologically driven groups," but their primary identification was with fellow professional aid workers. This story is consistent with the depiction of NGO workers as an "epistemic community of well-trained professionals." Ethnographers studying NGO workers have characterized the NGO scene as "Aidland"; they describe a circuit of aid workers moving among NGOs, government agencies, and for-profit contractors.[22] This easy movement is possible because the professionalization of NGOs has made public and private aid organizations *isomorphic*—they operate in similar ways and demand the same qualifications of their employees.[23] Monika Krause has shown how both competitive and normative pressures shape the professional field of humanitarian organizations. She found that while the desk workers of large NGOs did hold high ideals, in day-to-day reality their work was shaped by the need to produce "good projects" that could meet the demands of funding agencies.[24] NGOs, in this portrayal, make sense not when we view them as pure do-gooders but as actors operating within an organizational field shaped at once by ideals, competition for resources, and shared assumptions about the appropriate ways to do development.

Globalization Intervenes

This professionalization of NGOs has rightly attracted a good deal of attention from social scientists. But meanwhile globalization has been transforming the way that everyday citizens of developed countries encounter the Global South.[25] Global changes in transportation and electronic communication have simultaneously created new social problems (or made old ones newly visible) and provided novel tools to confront them. The result is new forms of organizations and activism that are driven more by networks than membership, and more by personal tastes and talents than by collective identities and consensus. The internet provides a platform for research, disseminating messages, organizing events, moving money, and administering projects on the other side of the globe—all tasks that required brick-and-mortar organizations thirty years ago. Thus liberated, "well-meaning amateurs" can now choose their targets and tailor the action to their personal tastes.

Other domains of activism and charity signal how globalization transforms ways of organizing. "Connective action" and political consumerism, like grassroots INGOs, move away from the state as a target of activism, reduce the role of traditional organizations, and elevate the role of personal, expressive action.[26] The Occupy protests, Black Lives Matter, the Indignados movement of Spain, the umbrella protest in Hong Kong, and the Putting People First campaign all fit the latter template. Membership organizations had small or invisible roles in all of these protests. Digital platforms like Twitter took up the role of coordinating action and spreading messages. But instead of the painstakingly wrought frames that bring together traditional collective action, *connective* action is motivated by looser messages that can be personalized and sent out by individuals. Political consumerism—the boycott of some goods and the "buycott" of others, based on political, environmental, or ethical concerns—is another domain where globalization has created new opportunities for personalized action. A number of labeling and certification schemes have emerged in recent decades to let shoppers know what social good they are doing with their purchase. A cup of coffee could be certified as Fair Trade, guaranteeing living wages and safe work conditions; as USDA Organic, eliminating synthetic pesticides; or as Bird-Friendly, promising that the coffee is grown in an area with a sufficient number and variety of shade trees. While the mingling of consumption and politics is nothing new, globalization has expanded the range of products that are sold while extending and obscuring the commodity chains. Commodities flow easily across borders, but regulations do not; the ability of the state to regulate how goods are produced has not kept pace with the complexity of global production.[27] Consumers can turn to certifying organizations to tell them about the virtues of various products and loosely organized campaigns—some organized by traditional advocacy groups, others not—to alert them to labels that are tied to sweatshops, that engage in tax evasion, or that degrade the environment.[28]

These examples show us that globalization creates new opportunities for charity and activism that allow everyday citizens to bypass or radically remake existing organizational forms. These forms of activism respond to problems that emerge or become suddenly visible when new products, information, and people begin to move across national borders. Traditional membership organizations play marginal roles, but as Schmitz and his colleagues argue, this does not indicate "a large-scale shift towards 'organizing without organizations.'"[29] Instead, we see new organizational forms where individualism is high and electronic communication allows small networks of passionate individuals to do the work that once required a bureaucracy.[30]

For Americans starting aid organizations, the most significant enabling change is the increasing number of ties to developing countries via migration and short-term travel. Thanks to the end of the Cold War and various civil wars, whole swaths of Africa, Central America, and Asia opened up to tourists by the 1990s. This was also at the moment when the price of airline tickets was declining in real dollars and the income of white-collar Americans was increasing. The 1965 immigration reform had swelled the population of highly educated Chinese and Indian immigrants, who by the turn of the millennium had the means to travel back and forth to their countries of origin. Immigrants and tourists alike could communicate with acquaintances abroad as the reach of the internet and mobile phones extended first to cities and then to rural provinces. Cheap container shipping now allows small-budget organizations to move goods around the world, while they can send money online through wire services and apps.

Grassroots INGOs emerge from Americans' travel to the Global South. Most often the travel is related to tourism, study, or volunteer work through existing partnerships with universities or civic groups. In other cases Americans return to their foreign countries of birth, or those of adopted children or immigrant spouses. Americans' aid projects often begin as a way of assisting specific communities encountered during these travels. This is a critical point: grassroots aid does not trickle down from a national development scheme, and it is rarely an innovation in search of apt "sites" for implementation. Instead, aid emerges in a personal, relational context.

With these relationships in place, Americans do not turn to seasoned development professionals for advice. (That the advice of experts on development has so often changed provides further encouragement to "commonsense" approaches.) Instead, they look to the playbook of civic life back home to structure new organizations, and they use stories of American success as blueprints for individual transformation in developing countries.

What This Book Is About

Blue Marble Dreams and the ten thousand organizations like it show that the NGO form is being reinvented as a vehicle for expressive personal charity. *Expressive*, *personal*, and *charity* are not words that most observers would use to describe the NGO field at large. In the 1980s, David Korten tracked the evolution of mainstream NGOs from dealing with the symptoms of poverty toward the causes—that is, a movement away from charitable approaches.[31] (Social enterprise, another new movement in private aid, tends to eschew the notion of charity in favor of harnessing profit motives for social value.[32]) And the dominant perspective of analyzing NGOs as members of a technocratic professional field turns attention away from expressive and personal characteristics. This perspective is useful for understanding organizational behavior. But it leaves in the shadows the moral and expressive forces that drive the creation of NGOs, and it keeps us from seeing how those forces evolve into new forms of action as technological and political realities change.

Just as globalization made possible connective action and political consumerism, so is it allowing well-intentioned amateurs to reinvent NGOs. Theories of nonprofit origins are useful to understand grassroots INGOs' emergence. First, these theories point us to both *demand-driven* and *supply-driven* explanations of the nonprofit sector, of which NGOs are a part. Demand-side theories explain the emergence of nonprofit organizations in response to government or market failures. But supply-side explanations remind us that, thanks to the relatively low bar to entry for nonprofits, the nonprofit sector is hospitable to "ideological entrepreneurs" who wish to provide services inflected by a particular set of values.[33] Peter Frumkin argues that the potential for individuals to use an organization to enact their ideas of the good life is in fact one of the constitutive qualities of the nonprofit sector.[34] It is part of a classically liberal conception of civil society that organizations can define and pursue different notions of the good. Grassroots INGOs, founded by energetic individuals with a particular vision—that might involve a flourishing small business or Christian fellowship or universal primary education—are best understood as supply driven.

But we can also distinguish between *instrumental* and *expressive* rationales for nonprofit action.[35] While an instrumental assessment of the nonprofit sector prizes efficient delivery of services, an expressive perspective sees distinct value in the way that the people involved in the organization experience fellowship or satisfaction even if efficiency is sacrificed. People can derive satisfaction from the very act of supporting a chosen cause—the arts, youth empowerment, the advancement of one's alma mater—regardless of the outcome.[36] Looking at nonprofits this way implies that nonprofits exist not simply because they can operate on low margins or because they generate public trust. From this perspective the nonprofit sector is unique because it offers emotional and moral possibilities unavailable through the state or market. The chapters ahead will show that the *expressive* quality of grassroots INGOs and the emotional valence of the work are critical to understanding these groups. This is important, because most analysts of nonprofit organizations that provide services assume that the instrumental rationale of the groups takes precedence. Most grassroots INGOs provide services of some type, but the Americans involved with these organizations derive deep emotional satisfaction (and sometimes frustration) from their efforts. Allowing expressive impulses to flourish in an NGO requires certain accommodations. It means allowing in foreign volunteers, even if it isn't particularly efficient to do so; choosing interventions that are of interest to Americans; and constantly negotiating between outsiders' ideas and insiders' practical knowledge.

Grassroots INGOs are *personal* in several senses of the term. First, individuals can be untethered from the traditional channels that might have supported them in their aid work: large INGOs, national aid agencies, denominational religious missions. Journalists writing about the emergence of volunteer-driven aid projects have recognized this personal dimension by dubbing them "DIY foreign aid" or "My Own NGO."[37] But the distinction between "personal" and "solo" is important. The energy of the individuals who start grassroots INGOs is a crucial part of their story, but to portray them as working alone is misleading. They draw on resources from their *personal networks* to support their work. Friends and family form the core of financial support and volunteer labor. Grassroots INGO founders turn to these people when they need to learn how to incorporate their organization, build a website, or run a fundraiser. They find support among coworkers and fellow members of religious congregations and other civic organizations. Grassroots INGO volunteers' work is shaped by repertoires of action from their personal lives. They draw not on discourse or skills learned from professional aid work, but from other domains. They use the language of "barn-raising" or draw on religious metaphors and raise money through the yard sales, golf outings, and silent auctions they have attended for other causes.

Second, the organizations are structured and aid is given in ways that emphasize *personal relationships* between aid givers and aid receivers. Grassroots INGOs give amateurs an opportunity that is unmatched elsewhere: to do hands-on work on projects of their own design. Grassroots INGOs can form around the tastes and talents of their leaders. Often leaders draw on ideas of what has made them—or their forebears—successful: education, vocational skills, or religious practices. They usually structure the organization to allow direct contact with aid recipients. This shapes not just the types of projects the leaders choose, but also the relationship between the organization and the community it aims to serve. Grassroots INGOs tend to rely on relationships with the same local partners for executing projects, enjoying emotional intimacy, and providing accountability. This provides grassroots INGOs with a great deal of flexibility, but the contradictions of these multiple roles also create hazards.

Grassroots INGOs' emphasis on personal relationships leads most of them to do work that is ultimately charity—that aims to improve individual lives but does little to change broader contexts. I show that while some grassroots INGOs provide goods and services and others focus on changing recipients' skills and dispositions, these approaches have in common an idea of "development" as individual transformation. Some grassroots INGOs strive to build organizations that have robust local governance (e.g., cooperatives) or that are integrated into existing institutions (for example, medical training overseen by the Ministry of Health). But because of the limited time many grassroots INGO leaders spend overseas, their lack of language skills and cultural competence, and their preference for emotionally satisfying encounters, many grassroots INGOs struggle to be integrated into local institutions of government and civic life. Nearly all avoid politics.

Grassroots INGOs are part of what the Indian anthropologist Arjun Appardurai describes as a shift from the "megarhetoric of development" to "micronarratives" that rewrite development "more as vernacular globalization and less as a concession to large-scale national and international policies."[38] Once we know that globalization transforms ways of organizing, a crucial task is understanding the nature of the new organizations. That is the aim of this book. In the chapters ahead I draw on in-depth studies of five grass-roots INGOs, documents from hundreds more, and IRS records from the universe of registered American relief, development, and human rights NGOs. I explain the emergence of these groups and describe the goods that their leaders work for, the places they work, the other actors they partner with, and the way they depict their beneficiaries to fellow Americans. I show that building NGOs around personal relationships and expressive rationales frees them from many of the pressures of the professionalized NGO field. But it also generates weak accountability to the people the groups aim to help and risks, as one grassroots INGO leader admitted, "re-inventing the wheel."[39]

NGOs are no longer the province of experts. I show that the tremendous growth of grassroots INGOs makes sense not in the narrow context of the aid field, but set against broader political and charitable movements for global change. By looking at the relationship between globalization and private aid from this perspective, we see how new NGOs find space to resist professionalization and to carry out programs and moral agendas that are much more diverse than recent scholarship has claimed.

I use the term *amateurs* in the book's title in a way that has already been suggested: to designate those who are outside the epistemic community of development experts.[40] But the term has other connotations. It suggests certain limits of skill or sophistication in a discipline: *mere amateurs*. Amateurism is theorized as one of the fundamental weaknesses of the nonprofit sector; Salamon describes a tendency of nonprofit organizations to fall back on "moral suasion" when they do not have the funds to hire professional workers with more refined skills.[41] But the term's Latin root—*amator*, or lover—points to motivation. An amateur is one who is motivated by the love of the game, for whom "the process is every bit as important as the outcome."[42] To refer to the people involved in grassroots INGOs as amateurs is also to refer to this expressive quality. In analyzing these groups, we should take seriously, if critically, the desire of everyday Americans to use NGOs as a tool do good in the world.

Data on Grassroots International NGOs and Chapter Overview

How best to study grassroots INGOs? Trying to make sense of a new social phenomenon bears a resemblance to the Indian fable of the blind men who tried to describe an elephant. One man, grasping the tusk, said the elephant was like a plowshare. Another touched the tail and said the elephant was like a rope, while others, grasping different parts, said the elephant was like a fan, a pillar, or a tree branch. In the happy version of the fable, the men share their knowledge and establish a picture of the entire beast. By a series of close-ups they are able to "see the elephant." My approach to making sense of grassroots INGOs has been slightly different. I use snapshots at different focal lengths: the landscape, the medium-range view, and the close-up. Every "snapshot" relies on a different source of data, each representing a distinct tradeoff of detail and scope.[43]

Enumerating NGOs is a notoriously difficult task. Scholars have relied on various combinations of shoe-leather searches, NGO registries, snowball sampling, and international directories, with no approach yielding a comprehensive list in any country or project domain.[44] Most of these approaches have special difficulty identifying small organizations. But looking at organizations headquartered in the United States offers the advantage of IRS records; any organization that raises $5,000 or more per year is, in principle, required to register with the agency. My "landscape" view of grassroots INGOs is the listing of 501(c)3 organizations coded by the IRS as International Relief, Development, or Human Rights organizations. Choosing this landscape excludes what Watkins and colleagues call "free-floating altruists," individuals doing aid work without a registered organization.[45] Were there some systematic way of finding and counting these individuals, the grassroots aid movement would be even larger in numbers and more varied in scope than I describe here. As it is, the IRS data, published by the National Center for Charitable Statistics at the Urban Institute, included records for 10,624 active US-based relief, development, and human rights organizations by the end of 2011.[46] This is the universe of organizations I consider in the book, though the number has grown since that time to over 13,000. These data also offer a considerable advantage over efforts to study volunteer-driven aid groups based in other developed countries, which typically have less robust systems for registering charitable organizations.

The medium-range perspective uses grassroots INGOs' own websites. IRS records say nothing about where international aid organizations work or the projects they undertake. While large NGOs issue annual reports, this is rare among smaller organizations. Most grassroots INGOs are not yet connected to the umbrella organizations that can provide data on the sector.[47] Using websites is the most effective means to gather basic information on the programs of a probability sample of organizations.

The strengths of website data are their ubiquity and orientation toward the interested public.[48] Since the sites are designed to inform prospective supporters, they typically include data on the types and locations of the organizations' projects. Narrative accounts of the work and "About Us" and "Get Involved" pages yield other sorts of information—on the roles that potential supporters can play, and the organizational partners already connected to the INGO. Accounts of projects and fundraising events and other pages that name "partners" reveal a host of network connections: other NGOs, businesses, religious congregations, government agencies, and civic groups. Web pages are also rich sites of symbolic action; texts about how projects work, who benefits from them, and why NGOs engage in them reveal a good deal about NGOs' notions of what constitutes "good aid."[49] Here I draw on a random sample of 150 websites from the universe of 6,564 functioning websites run by the 10,624 active organizations registered with the IRS.

Finally, to get at the deeper questions of how grassroots INGO leaders understand their work and the ways they mediate between communities in the United States and the Global South, I analyze five case study organizations. I selected these groups to vary in budget, project sector, and US location, but all operate in East Africa, a common destination region for grassroots INGOs. I interviewed the founder and current board members of each of these organizations, reviewed internal and public-facing documents, and visited their project sites abroad. This involved trips to Michigan, Texas, Massachusetts, and Minnesota, where I spent time at kitchen tables, company cafeterias, and church lobbies. I also visited the communities where these organizations work in Kenya, Uganda, Rwanda, and Tanzania. During my time with each organization I spent days with the local brokers—typically paid employees who keep the projects running day to day. I observed projects and spoke with the people using the workshops, schools, and hospitals these grassroots INGOs support. I shadowed a number of volunteers and observed what those intense weeks of their lives are like when they step off a plane in Nairobi or Dar es Salaam and into an East African clinic or school. The names of these five organizations and the individuals associated with them are pseudonyms. The exception is Indego Africa and its two founders, Matt Mitro and Ben Stone, who agreed to be named because of previous published work on the organization. I discuss my data and methods in greater depth in a note at the end of the book.

Chapter Overview

Chapter 1 introduces the five case study organizations. For Kenya's Tomorrow is an organization that works in the slums of Nairobi and was founded by a young Pentecostal woman from Michigan who eventually married the son of her Kenyan aid counterpart. Indego Africa works with women artisans in Rwanda, and the Rwanda Ultrasound Initiative was started by two emergency medicine residents to bring US doctors to African hospitals as teacher-trainers. Wellsprings of Hope was founded by a self-described "cowboy-pastor" and operates schools, clinics, and child sponsorship programs in Uganda. Activate Tanzania was started by a Tanzanian immigrant to the United States who was the first person in his village to go to high school.

We will see that the people who launched these groups vary in their education, race, religiosity, and politics. The vignettes show how the global ties that have become common among the American middle class set the stage for new aid efforts. I show how founders decide whom to aid and how to do it, with implications that emerge in chapters 3–6.

After the close-up on five organizations in chapter 1, chapter 2 zooms out to provide a quantitative description of the foreign locations, project sectors, targeted recipients, and roles for US supporters of grassroots international NGOs. To highlight the distinctive character of grassroots aid, I contrast these findings with the patterns of official development assistance distributed by USAID. The chapter draws on a content analysis of 150 websites randomly selected from active organizations in IRS records (operationally defining those founded in 1990 or later and with annual income of $250,000 or less as grassroots INGOs). These are the first published descriptive statistics from a nationally representative sample of American grassroots INGOs.

Chapter 3 uses the website and case study data to analyze how grassroots INGOs understand the process of development and how those understandings shape the ways they carry out aid work. In the past four decades the increasing professionalization of international development made it harder for everyday Americans to be involved in mainstream forms of aid. But Americans had opportunities to build ties to developing countries through other means, as migrants arrived, Americans traveled, and people could communicate cheaply across international borders. Grassroots INGOs have emerged to allow well-intentioned amateurs to be involved in ways that are now impossible through traditional channels of aid: they can work directly with beneficiaries, share their own vocational skills, and use their own histories of social mobility as blueprints for development.

Chapter 4 lays out grassroots INGOs' approach to aid and considers how it is distinctive from aid as practiced by mainstream NGOs in the past or present. I develop a typology with three models of aid: the first focusing on direct provision of goods and services, the second on skills and dispositions, and the third on social relations. These aid approaches are satisfying for American supporters because they can observe that material needs have been met or that aid recipients have acquired new educational credentials or work skills. Yet the emphasis on provision of goods and services—that is, welfare provision—casts grassroots INGOs in a role that NGO experts had rejected as outdated by the 1980s.

The personal networks of globalization make grassroots INGOs viable, and chapters 5 and 6 elaborate on relationships between founders and associates in aid-receiving communities (chapter 5) and with their friends and family at home in the United States (chapter 6). Both types of relationships have profound consequences for the establishment, maintenance, and influence of grassroots INGOs. Loved ones in the Global South often provide the motivation for Americans to launch aid projects, and these trusted associates often become the organizations' brokers—the channel through which Americans assess local development problems and opportunities, and gauge the impact of their work. I argue that this way of structuring an NGO provides flexibility but weak downward accountability, and point to ways that grassroots INGOs can address this weakness.

Meanwhile, American leaders draw on their social networks for resources to support their organizations, and in these interactions transmit their ideas about poverty and development. Given most Americans' scant knowledge of the Global South, grassroots INGO leaders' arguments have particular credibility; their accounts are trusted by family and friends, and moreover, they've "seen it with their own eyes." I show the ways that supporters of grassroots INGOs transmit their ideas about development to fellow Americans. Their discourse rouses compassion, but limits the images of people in the Global South to being aid recipients and Americans to being the agents of change.

Chapter 7 considers the role of religion in grassroots INGOs. The United States is highly religious compared with other aid-giving countries, and religion shapes even grassroots INGOs that do not label themselves as "religious" or "faith-based." Religion offers a case of *how* personal relationships are converted into the resources needed for development work. I show that leaders selectively draw on three kind of religious resources: *frames* for explaining and justifying their work, *modes of voluntary action* from people's religious lives, and *networks* of people in congregations and denominations that provide the resources that small-budget groups need to survive.

The conclusion summarizes the findings and turns to the question of how we should assess these organizations. Doing development as a personal charity has consequences for the communities that receive aid and the Americans who give it. Grassroots INGOs allow Americans to pursue the morally worthy goal of alleviating poverty, and it permits them to use their time and skills in ways that are impossible elsewhere in the aid world. These organizations have other advantages: they are insulated from the pressures that professionalized NGOs face to quantify their results and to create projects that can be replicated. But "thinking small" does not avoid all of the problems of private aid. Grassroots INGOs struggle to raise funds, to be accountable to recipients, and to integrate themselves into local institutions that could make their work sustainable. Pursuing expressive goals while directly providing services, as most grassroots INGOs do, is fraught. At worst, this can compromise the well-being of aid recipients to satisfy the desires of volunteers. And by depicting development as a problem of individual economic mobility, grassroots INGOs allow supporters to ignore broader struggles of politics, climate change, and the globalized economy. The chapters that follow show the aspirations and limits of personal compassion on a global scale.

I turn first to the stories of six Americans—Erasto, Natalie, Bill, Megan, Tamara, and Matt—and how their ties to Africa evolved into grassroots INGOs.

1   *Origin Stories*

Before we can make sense of how grassroots INGOs are remaking development aid, we need to understand how these organizations start. This chapter tells five groups' origin stories. These organizations were established between 2000 and 2010 by Americans with different sorts of links to Africa—some the loose ties of previous volunteer work, but some the more intimate bonds of migration or marriage. The founder of the first group I describe was born in Tanzania and migrated to the United States in his twenties; in his thirties, he launched a grassroots INGO to aid his native village. A second group was started by an American who had spent several childhood years in West Africa but went on to start an organization in Rwanda. Three of the groups were started by Americans who had done short-term volunteer work in Africa, sometimes in countries other than those where they launched their grassroots INGO. We see that cooperation among family members is a common feature of these organizations and that religion often plays roles in motivating or facilitating these organizations' births—a theme I develop further in chapter 7.

    If the ability to be a short-term volunteer is one of the novelties of working with a grassroots INGO—nineteenth-century missionaries were understood to have committed for the remainder of their lives—another novelty is the ability to do aid work part-time. Three of the organizations were launched as part-time ventures, and the leaders of the remaining two, Indego Africa and For Kenya's Tomorrow, scaled back to part-time involvement within several years of founding. Recent scholarship on full-time aid workers has shown that even professional aid workers do not have tidy identities that separate their work from the rest of their lives; they are constantly working to integrate their personal sense of self into new surroundings and jobs that are physically demanding and emotionally exhausting.[1] But as these vignettes show, the task is different for the founders of grassroots INGOs. These individuals are building the identity of "aid worker" *around* their other identities and learning what it means to do development work in the context of their families or within religious or professional networks. The leaders of these groups have kept one foot in the world of their American careers and personal lives, and the other in the world of their African friendships and projects.

The groups' origin stories given below highlight the diversity of these worlds. Table 1 gives a few basic details of each group's operation.

Activate Tanzania

Until Activate Tanzania started work in 2004, you could count on your fingers the number of people from Muyinga who had gone to secondary school.[2] One of those was Erasto, who then became the first from the village to attend college in the United States. As a student at a Lutheran liberal arts college, he met a fellow student named Kate, from Minnesota, who was studying anthropology and

TABLE 1. Case Study Organizations

Organization	US Base	International Base	Main Project(s)	Annual Revenue[a]
Activate Tanzania	St. Paul, Minnesota	Village in Tanzania	Secondary school	$79,498
For Kenya's Tomorrow (FKT)	Rural Michigan	Nairobi, Kenya	Sanitation, microenterprise	~$20,000
Wellsprings of Hope	Suburb of San Antonio, Texas	Large town in Uganda	Religious mission, primary schools, clinic	$189,888
Rwanda Ultrasound Initiative (RUI)	Boston	Rwanda (various hospitals)	Ultrasound training for Rwandan doctors	~$10,000
Indego Africa	New York City	Rwanda (Kigali and smaller towns)	Women's microenterprise	$457,297

[a] 501(c)3 organizations with less than $50,000 in revenue are not required to report an exact amount to the IRS with their annual Form 990 filing. Their revenues are recorded by the IRS as $0. The revenue figures here were from given to me in interviews by the presidents of For Kenya's Tomorrow and the Rwanda Ultrasound Initiative. Note that by the end of the period of my research, Indego's annual revenue exceeded the $250,000 ceiling used to operationally define grassroots INGOs in other parts of the book. Yet, as this chapter describes, Indego Africa's origins are incontestably grassroots. I elected to retain Indego in the book so that readers can see one possible trajectory of the growth of a grassroots INGO.

had traveled to Cameroon and Nepal. They returned to her hometown and married, and soon Erasto found a job in software engineering. Before long, Kate and Erasto welcomed two sons. During these years Erasto occasionally returned to Tanzania and often sent cash to support his extended family there. Erasto and Kate quickly found support in Minnesota when they first broached the idea of opening a secondary school in his home village.

One of the legacies of German colonial rule in Tanzania was the presence of Lutheran churches, which throughout the twentieth century grew with support from European and American missionaries. It was through these relationships that Erasto had won a scholarship to study in the United States, and these Lutheran ties also linked St. Paul, Minnesota, to Erasto's home region of Tanzania through a sister-church relationship that began in the early 1990s. Through friends, Erasto was introduced to a Lutheran pastor who had traveled several times to Tanzania; they soon discovered that the pastor had not only visited Erasto's village, but had also met his mother.

These religious ties notwithstanding, the objective of Activate Tanzania from the beginning was secular and specific: to open a private secondary school in Muyinga. As an immigrant who had made good, Erasto had for many years been seen as a patron of his village, and ultimately, he wanted to do something other than give ad hoc donations in response to individual requests. Students in Tanzania are admitted to secondary school on the basis of competitive examinations and even in public schools must pay fees. For Erasto, being admitted to secondary school was the turning point in life, and he believed that better access to education would do more good for the village than anything else he could contribute.

Starting in 2004, Erasto and Kate approached their friends, colleagues, fellow church members, and her large extended family for donations to build the school. Erasto's boyhood friend, still living in Tanzania, brokered a deal with the village leadership: the school would take possession of several empty buildings and a tract of land owned by the village government, and in exchange the school would provide ten full-tuition scholarships each year for village children. Within about a year, Erasto and Kate had raised $80,000. Renovation on the buildings began—with the money being wired through the Saint Paul Lutheran Synod, since Erasto and Kate had not yet set up a 501(c)3—and the Muyinga Secondary School opened for its first students in 2006.

Back in Minnesota, the school project had attracted particular interest from working and retired teachers. Consensus emerged among Erasto, Kate, and the newly formed board that the Muyinga school should exceed typical Tanzanian standards of education. While adhering to requirements of the Tanzanian national curriculum, the school should instill the American educational values of creativity and problem solving. The board believed the school would need good facilities like a library and science lab if students were to do more than learn by rote; in addition, they would need to lure good teachers with competitive salaries. Erasto played the middle man, having final say on issues of spending and personnel in Tanzania, trying to relay the American board's vision to Tanzanian school leadership while also sensitizing Americans to long-held Tanzanian ways of doing things.

Board members and other supporters made trips to visit the school roughly every other year beginning in 2006. While visiting, they assisted in English classes and offered in-service training to the Muyinga teachers. Three recent US college graduates have now served as volunteer teachers for a semester or more at the school. The school has posted strong test scores on the national exam and has been able to attract highly qualified teachers who had taught in other private schools in Tanzania. Now that the school has two hundred students and about two dozen employees, Activate Tanzania has to bear all of the challenges of operating a selective private school (teacher complaints about salary and living space; parents late on their tuition payments) while operating a 501(c)3 that can continue to appeal to volunteers and donors to raise the tens of thousands of dollars the school requires in excess of tuition receipts to stay open each year. These responsibilities obligate Erasto to spend late-night hours on the phone to Tanzania several days a week. He jokes that he is "a programmer by day but teacher by night."

For Kenya's Tomorrow

For Kenya's Tomorrow is the product of the extraordinary energy of a young Pentecostal woman from rural Michigan. After growing up in a church that supported several missionaries and taking a religious volunteer trip herself to Malawi as a fifteen-year-old, Natalie was living in Florida, in a young marriage that was dissolving, and wondering if she could "get Africa out of [her] heart." An acquaintance at her church in Florida gave her the name of a man working with a church-based community organization in the Nairobi slum of Kawangare, and in 2008 Natalie flew to Kenya to see what she could do there. Natalie's previous volunteer work in Malawi had given her the idea to work with AIDS orphans or street children, but on this trip, she had a visceral reaction to the sanitation conditions in the slum and decided that she would focus her work there. She explained this shift in focus as divine intervention:

I just had this vision flash before my eyes of just a place that didn't exist at the current time. It was, you know, pure streams where sewage was running and where there was trash everywhere. . . . And so, when I got that vision, it literally like slapped me on the back of the head because I had never, never envisioned doing anything like that. My heart was really to be with AIDS orphans, and street children, and all that. And so, since obviously my relationship with God plays into this a lot, I really just started seeking God and said, "What does this look like to you? Where did this come from? Because I don't know what to do with it." And then I just really got some clarity with addressing the sanitation issues and what that looked like with toilets and with new shower rooms and recycling centers, and addressing water issues and all of that. And then I just started kind of heading in that direction.

Having no professional training in development work generally or sanitation specifically (she had left college before completing a degree), Natalie returned to the United States and began her research at a Barnes and Noble bookstore and on the internet. In the same period, she recruited several peers to serve on the organization's board of directors: her sister, two childhood friends (one who worked at a bank, another with a degree in engineering), and two friends from her Florida church. To raise money, Natalie sent out a letter to friends and family explaining her project and asking for support. This sort of letter was not unusual among her circle of acquaintances—she had sent out a similar letter in the past, asking for financial support for her religious mission trip, and her family regularly made small contributions to others making similar requests. She gave a speech at the Michigan church she had attended as a girl, which her parents still attended, and the congregation agreed to add her to its roster of sponsored missionaries and make regular contributions to her work.

Natalie continued to travel to Kenya for a few months a year, seeking out partners for her sanitation projects. She made a crucial connection with Ruth, a Kenyan pastor who had founded a Pentecostal church in Kawangare that drew a few dozen worshippers each Sunday. Ruth was also the head of a community-based organization (CBO). This was crucial for Natalie's entrée into the community and for meeting Kenya's legal requirement that foreign NGOs partner with a local CBO. The other important consequence was that Natalie eventually came to date Ruth's son, David, a musician. Natalie and David married in 2011. Ruth and David's family and close friends became the trusted network upon which Natalie built the organization's work in Nairobi, while her own family and close friends provided financial and administrative support in the United States.

The sanitation projects moved slowly. Eager to see some tangible results, Natalie used a $10,000 donation to set up a workshop where a handful of Kawangare women could make beaded jewelry. This idea was modeled loosely on what Natalie had seen at fair trade shops in the United States, in particular, a Kenyan company called Kazuri Beads. Natalie took on the tasks of purchasing the beads, creating the designs and teaching them to the workers, and taking the bracelets back to the United States for sale. There was no grand scheme for the sale of these bracelets; they sold a few at a time to friends, and Natalie and some of the board members approached shops that they knew of and asked if they would carry them.

While the women's craft shop began operations and Natalie continued research on sanitation projects, she regularly began accepting "mission teams," or groups of short-term volunteers, from her Michigan church. These groups would participate in church services and Bible studies with Ruth's congregation and offer special prayer meetings in Kawangare; they also volunteered with the Saturday meals provided for children at Ruth's church. Though these teams' work was not connected intimately to the development projects that Natalie envisioned for For Kenya's Tomorrow (FKT), Natalie encouraged the trips because travelers often became committed supporters of the organization.

In 2012, FKT built its first two biogas toilets in Kawangare. The women's workshop was producing a small quantity of jewelry that was sold in the United States, and FKT paid for and staffed a "feeding," or lunch and playtime session, each Saturday at Ruth's church. Natalie and David, by then parents of a baby girl, worked full-time for FKT and split the year between their families' homes in Nairobi and Michigan. Much of the day-to-day work in Kenya was carried out by Martin, a childhood friend of David's. FKT is pursuing a small grant from the Rotary Club, but continues to rely on a handful of Pentecostal congregations in the United States and the individual donations of family and friends for its operating funds.

Wellsprings of Hope

Founded by a self-described Baptist "cowboy-pastor," Wellsprings of Hope is a Christian organization operated in Uganda by a group of five pastors and in the United States by a cadre of volunteers drawn from Baptist, Methodist, and nondenominational evangelical churches in suburban San Antonio. Shared religious faith is at the heart of the organization. The partnership began when Pastor Bill Smith visited Uganda with a delegation of Baptist preachers, and the initial goal was to provide financial support for the "ministry" of five Ugandan pastors that he met there. Influenced by larger religious ministries in Uganda that were catering to earthly needs, the five pastors shared with Bill their ambitions that extended beyond preaching the gospel: schools, clinics, youth programs. Bill's US congregation agreed to send money, and soon the volunteers followed. By 2006, teams of volunteers from Bill's congregation and from the town's United Methodist Church were coming to Uganda for multiweek stints.

Uganda has been heavily evangelized in the last three decades, particularly by conservative Protestant groups, but the town where Wellsprings of Hope is based maintains a slight Muslim majority. Surprise at the harmonious relationships between Christian and Muslim Ugandans was a recurring note in my conversations with the Texas volunteers. With the steady financial contributions of the Texans, Wellsprings of Hope now operates two elementary schools, a clinic, men's and women's religious ministries (which include Bible teaching and vocational training), and a farm. The five pastors serve as directors for all these programs and oversee the nurse who runs the clinic and the headmasters of both schools. This is a source of some tension, because in Uganda nurse and school headmaster are prestige positions, and the pastors have less education than these professionals.

Most of the American board members of Wellsprings are retirees from long careers in related fields—nursing, teaching, accounting, and construction—and as a result they have strong ideas about how the organization should operate in Uganda. These ideas are borne out in what the board members believe should be the material standards in the clinic and schools and priorities in how money should be spent. But differences in opinion between the American and

Ugandan leadership are smoothed by the mutual good feelings engendered by the frequent (yearly or twice-yearly) visits of many of the board members to Uganda, and by what both Ugandans and Texans explain as a common purpose that emerges from their shared faith. Wellsprings' most consistent source of revenue is monthly child sponsorships. Wellsprings introduced this model after seeing it gainfully used by Africa Renewal Ministries, another evangelical NGO based in San Antonio and operating in Uganda. American sponsors contribute $35 to $50 a month, with the bulk of that providing for school fees and uniforms, and the rest kept in a reserve fund to pay for medical expenses or other family difficulties. The approximately 150 child sponsorships organized by Wellsprings are one of the major channels through which some relationship is forged between Ugandans and Americans. Sponsored children are required to write letters to their sponsors at least twice a year, and the younger students (for whom English is a second or third language) do so with the help of a teacher or social worker. American sponsors receive a photograph of their sponsored child every year, and in some cases, copies of the students' school report cards. The American coordinator of the sponsorships, Frances, explains, "[I send] any piece of information I can get because I want the sponsors to know their kids as individuals, not just a name. I want them to know what their struggles are and whether they're doing well in school or not, and what they need to be praying for, for that child." The sponsorship program is therefore not just a reliable source of revenue for the organization, but also a key site where ideas of Ugandans are shaped and transmitted by the organization to American supporters.

These personal relationships and shared religious beliefs are what Wellsprings of Hope's supporters value most in the organization and see as the qualities that distinguish it from other aid organizations. But as the organization approaches two hundred sponsored children and seventy-five Ugandans on the payroll—from the pastors down to the janitor of the clinic—the financial and organizational demands of the organization are prodding it toward increased formalization. The Ugandan pastors have been trained to keep financial spreadsheets and to submit them each month to the US treasurer. American volunteers value the fact that most of the money they raise goes directly to Ugandans, but the burden of voluntary labor is heavy. One former board member explained,

> With an all-volunteer organization I think that's tough as well because we're a working board. It's not a board that gets together once a month . . . and I think that takes a toll on the volunteers. I've often felt we needed to have a full-time bookkeeper/fundraiser/ all-accompanying person, but we don't have the funds to support that, and we don't want to take out of our sponsorship dollars because they're doing such a vital need in Uganda. . . . I know it's being spent for the ministry. They're not buying cars and they're not buying all fancy stuff. They're all living pretty humble lives. And when you get to see the kids firsthand it's a big difference.

Wellsprings' primary challenge as of this writing is maintaining the close "personal relationships" that American volunteers emphasized repeatedly in interviews despite the logistical realities of an increasingly complex aid organization.

Rwanda Ultrasound Initiative (RUI)

If shared religious faith is at the heart of Wellsprings of Hope's work in East Africa, the shared professional identity of "physician" is at the heart of the Rwanda Ultrasound Initiative. The project uses American doctors to train their Rwandan counterparts to use ultrasound as a broad diagnostic tool. While the ultimate beneficiaries are Rwandan patients, the immediate targets of RUI's work are doctors. During their training visits, American doctors have little contact with Rwandan patients; they perform few medical procedures themselves, but instead observe and coach Rwandan doctors using the American model of clinical medical education.

From the beginning, RUI collaborated with the Rwandan Ministry of Health to devise a curriculum that would fit into the ministry's broad national scheme to improve medical education. The Rwandan health care system is centralized, so the Ministry of Health assigns doctors to hospitals or clinics. RUI not only had to seek certification for its curriculum, but had to reach consensus with the government over which hospitals they would target for training and the amount of in-service time that the doctor-trainees would be granted. RUI convened eighteen Rwandan physicians for a two-week intensive training in Kigali in fall 2012. In the following five months, pairs of American doctors came to Rwanda in two-week shifts to supervise the doctor-trainees using their new diagnostic techniques. Most of the American doctors came from emergency medicine departments and had learned about the RUI volunteer opportunity through the email lists of the American College of Emergency Physicians. RUI provided some teaching materials and local cell phones; it was up to the American volunteers to finance their own travel.

The Rwanda Ultrasound Initiative was launched by two American emergency medicine residents. Megan brought the Rwanda connection; she had studied there for several months as part of a medical school exchange. Tamara, a resident physician at

Massachusetts General and Brigham and Women's Hospitals in Boston, had been part of several overseas medical volunteer trips—including a relief mission to Haiti just after the 2010 earthquake. The medical teams there, lacking a laboratory and more sophisticated medical imaging, used ultrasound machines to diagnose a variety of injuries. Tamara returned to the United States convinced that ultrasound, which was also being increasingly used in American emergency departments, could be a useful diagnostic tool in places where medical infrastructure was limited. She approached Julia, her supervising physician, who was active in professional groups engaged in initiatives to bring point-of-care ultrasound into broader use in American hospitals. Julia connected Megan and Tamara and put them in touch with an international ultrasound project, WINFOCUS, which became a source for some of the training materials that RUI would eventually use. Megan used her connections in Rwanda to negotiate with the Ministry of Health, and Tamara also traveled to Rwanda to assess the ultrasound equipment that was available in the district hospitals and how it was being used. She found that most of the district hospitals had ultrasound machines, but that they were only used only for obstetrics or not at all.

In the remainder of 2011 and in the early months of 2012, Megan tended to the nuts and bolts of the organization. She found a group of law students at the University of Pennsylvania who were willing to file the paperwork to have RUI recognized as a tax-exempt 501(c)3. Another emergency medicine physician friend of Megan's was part of a web startup, Good Works Global, that aims to connect potential donors with NGOs. RUI raised some funds through the site but found most of their donations by reaching out to friends and family through letters and Facebook posts. Megan secured a

$10,000 grant from a small foundation in spring 2012, and both doctors' hospitals offered them small donations to offset their travel expenses. Both Megan and Tamara continued their back-breaking work schedules as residents while navigating a back-and-forth with Rwandan officials that barely concluded in time to launch the training program in September 2012. In early 2013, Julia told me that they considered the fall 2012 training to be a qualified success. Whether they would continue to offer training programs, however, depended on better cooperation from the Rwandan government as well as the activities of larger, better-funded medical education projects. Brigham and Women's Hospital—where Julia and Tamara were based—had just been named a recipient of a multimillion-dollar grant from the Doris Duke Foundation aimed at improving medical training in Rwanda, which threatened to make RUI's projects redundant.

The accommodation was to offer a "train the trainers" program that allowed the Rwanda program to mainly become self-sufficient. Rwandan physicians trained by RUI would go on to train other physicians in the country. Meanwhile, Tamara and some new American volunteer physicians struck out to establish partnerships in other African countries. The model initially used in Rwanda of one-on-one training between American and local physicians was replicated in a large regional hospital in Uganda. An emergency medicine resident from the University of Pennsylvania, a native of Nigeria, led the effort to develop a small ultrasound training program on Zanzibar, in Tanzania. RUI operated at a steady annual budget of about $60,000, relying on American doctors to donate their labor and travel costs. Megan reduced her involvement in RUI over time but remained on the board. Tamara, on the other hand, stayed at the helm and began to build her professional identity around her work with the grassroots INGO. Now an attending physician in emergency medicine, she leads two international committees on global expansion of point-of-care ultrasound.

Indego Africa

The last organization I discuss at length, Indego Africa, is the most formalized of the five. While the bead bracelets crafted by For Kenya's Tomorrow's artisans are sold by the founder's sister to her fellow waitresses at Outback Steakhouse, Indego has landed retail contracts with Ralph Lauren, Nicole Miller, and J. Crew. Indego's sleek website displays jewelry, home accessories, and handbags crafted by six artisan co-ops in Rwanda. The New York office is run by an MBA as well as a lawyer with experience in the fashion industry, plus a host of interns. The Kigali office employs a Rwandan country director who was educated in Switzerland and the United States, three other Rwandan college graduates, and its own crop of American interns. "Social enterprise" was not part of the founder's vocabulary when he made his first moves to set up Indego in 2006, but the organization has come to be designated as such. Indego was a semifinalist for a grant from Echoing Green, a funder of social entrepreneurs, and in 2011 the organization was the subject of a Harvard Business School case study.

The $70 baskets sold in Indego's online store are woven by middle-aged Rwandan women. They come to work sometimes six days a week at the concrete block buildings their cooperatives have built or rented. The women sit straight-legged on mats on the floor in the common African fashion and weave the baskets while they chat in Kinyarwanda. A baby or toddler might accompany its mother, but one of the benefits of the Indego partnership that the women artisans happily report is an income sufficient to pay school fees for their children. Part of Indego's approach is to offer the artisans fair-trade pricing for their products. The organization's high-end marketing strategy allows them to charge premium prices for the handicrafts, but the major difference between Indego and a traditional production contract is that Indego pays the artisans half of the anticipated profits when the order is placed. This transfers much of the risk away from the Rwandan women—the party least able to afford it—and on to Indego and its retail partners.

This is the basic scheme imagined by Indego's founder, Matt Mitro, when he took the first steps to establish Indego in 2006. Matt had spent ages four to seven and eleven to fourteen in Lagos, Nigeria, where his father worked as an economist for an oil company. The issues of poverty and economic development were regular topics of conversation in Matt's expatriate family. After completing law school in the United States and working for two years at a firm in Washington, D.C., Matt was ambivalent about practicing law and made his first inquiries with family and friends about starting an NGO in Africa. Matt was favorably inclined toward entrepreneurial models of aid after encountering successful artisan projects in Africa and because of the influential perspective of his economist father. In Matt's view, projects that facilitate entrepreneurship are financially more sustainable than "service delivery" models, and are also more apt to transform the beneficiaries: "I think that the actual conduct of economic activity in business is really healthy. . . . I think that's a good experience for people's confidence. Obviously it's good for them in terms of being able to support themselves. . . . Taking risks I think generally is like a healthy thing for people to do. We thought this was the most easy way to facilitate that."

The early members of Indego's board included Matt's father and a family friend with a strong professional network in Rwanda. Though Rwanda strictly regulates the work of NGOs, the government is favorably disposed toward business approaches to aid and to foreign investment generally. The family friend's connections proved useful during a fact-finding trip to Rwanda, and Matt and the nascent Indego board decided to launch operations there. Soon after that 2007 visit, Indego had signed agreements with the two artisan co-ops, and Matt set out to locate retail buyers for the products. Consumed by the demands of setting up the retail partnerships, Matt soon approached a college friend, Ben Stone, also an attorney, to handle the legal requirements of an import-business-cum-nonprofit. The work was demanding, but also more appealing to Ben's professional interests than his work with a New York law firm had been. But Ben's supervisors at the law firm were eager to support Indego, and so they offered Ben a year's paid leave and continued use of office space. Ben held the role of Indego general counsel, and for some periods, COO and CEO, through July 2012.

The Indego board quickly came to realize that fair-trade pricing was not enough to help the artisan co-ops thrive as businesses. When Indego first established partnerships with two cooperatives in 2007, the sophistication of the groups differed widely. The Kigali-based group included women with some formal education and years of working together—they already had accounting schemes in place, although their management needed improvement. The other group, comprised of older women in a rural district, was a far looser configuration. Many of the women were illiterate and none had any experience with bookkeeping. Indego developed training materials for each group—basic literacy, numeracy, and bookkeeping for the less sophisticated organization, and more advanced training in cooperative governance, English, and computers for the more educated group. The delivery of the training programs constituted another social benefit. Indego partnered with Orphans of Rwanda (now Generation Rwanda), an NGO that offered college scholarships to genocide orphans and other vulnerable youth, to provide the training. The Orphans of Rwanda teaching interns received a stipend and marketable experience, while Indego gained talented and locally competent trainers for its programs. Two of the teaching interns were eventually hired as full-time staff in the Kigali office.

By the end of 2012, Matt and Ben had left full-time management of Indego in favor of a successor but remained as chairman and vice chairman of the board, respectively. Traditional fundraising contributed 60 percent of Indego's gross receipts in 2016. The organization hosted successful fundraising events in New York, Chicago, San Francisco, Los Angeles, and Washington, D.C., and its products were featured in *In Style*, *Marie Claire*, and *Architectural Digest*. But the sustainability of the organization depended on the continued willingness of highly educated staff to work for salaries well below the market rate. And while much of the popular appeal of Indego is its social enterprise model, Matt conceded that the approach was complex and expensive:

I think this is one of the biggest challenges that we face; it's like we're kind of running like four organizations at once. We're running a business in the US, definitely, like a sales business in the US. We're running a nonprofit and fundraising operation in the US. We're running a business supply chain operation in Rwanda. And we're running like a university in Rwanda. I mean, so doing that profitably and lucratively for people that work there, that may never work, to be honest. So, I don't count on the success yet because I don't know that that's ever going to really work.

By the standards of grassroots INGOs, Indego has been extraordinarily successful in its impact on beneficiaries, its fundraising, and its public recognition. The founder of the organization remains committed to Indego's hybrid model, even as he questions whether its complexity and high costs make the organization's success sustainable.

The case study snapshots offered here foreshadow several of the themes that emerge in later chapters: the role of personal networks in the launch of grassroots INGOs; the value placed on perceived intimacy between giver and receiver; and organizations' emphasis on providing not just goods, but also new skills and subjectivities to their recipients. The analysis of websites in the next chapter expands these themes by detailing precisely what sorts of projects grassroots INGOs undertake, where they operate, and how they describe the recipients.

2 *Who, What, Where?*

The Projects of Grassroots International NGOs

The last chapter's stories show how the personal relationships, interests, and skills of grassroots INGOs' founders play a decisive role in shaping the organizations. We have seen that the leaders of these groups are not aid experts, but remain embedded in their American lives with jobs, family, and religious congregations. They raise money from their friends and family using fundraising techniques they've learned from American civic life. They treasure the time they spend in their African host communities but rely on local partners to carry out work during most of the year. These qualities distinguish them from the traditional aid agencies about whom we know much more. This chapter moves beyond the case studies to a probabilistic sample of 150 grassroots INGOs to ask where these organizations work, what they do, and whom they serve. (A list of the organizations is in appendix 3.) This chapter provides the first systematic description of American grassroots INGOs' destinations, projects, intended recipients, and roles for volunteers.[1]

Finding systematic data about NGOs' locations and activities is a perennial problem for people who study the sector. The information about projects and programs contained in IRS filings is minimal, and few grassroots INGOs issue annual reports or provide data to umbrella organizations like InterAction. However, a majority of grassroots INGOs maintains websites. The percentage of grassroots INGOs with websites (61%) equals or exceeds typical survey response rates.[2] Websites also offer certain kinds of rich symbolic material that would be difficult to capture in a survey.[3] The sites contain photographs and personal accounts of trips to aid-receiving communities. When organizations describe their work on their websites, they often mention groups of targeted recipients like women or youth. NGOs describe the people they serve in terms of *status designations* (men, women, children, and so on) and in terms of *personal qualities*. Grassroots INGOs often include on their websites biographical narratives of individual recipients. These narratives, alongside accounts of the organization's work that include interactions with recipients, are sites for discourse about the character or nature of the recipients.[4]

I suggest that website texts describing even these status designations be interpreted as "intended" or "ideal" recipients, though there are likely to be spillover effects to other recipients. For example, a website that described distributing weekly food rations to Ugandan women would likely also benefit the men and children living in those households. Although the status designations are a reasonable account of the targeted recipients of a given aid organization, the website text should not be understood as some sort of objective audit. Texts about how projects work, who benefits from them, and why organizations engage in them reveal a good deal about grassroots INGOs' notions of what constitutes "good aid."

Besides characterizing recipients, website texts also offer rationales for their action. I define *rationales* as discursive acts that explain why something was done. Grassroots INGOs' websites often offer rationales for why particular people should be helped or why a particular intervention is appropriate. These are claims about moral deservedness, but they are also claims about the obligations of givers. Rationales are powerful as forms of persuasion only insofar as they align with existing logics of obligation. To use the metaphor of the recipient as child and the giver as parent builds on an accepted logic of parental obligation. Abstract principles of justice or rights can provide other logics, as can other relationships or forms of shared identity. Rationales differ from motivations in that we understand them to be an *account* of why something is done; to understand something as a rationale is to understand it as a speech act rather than as a motivation that is deep-seated within an individual.[5] The ways in which recipients are framed is particularly important for NGOs because of the vast social distance between the recipients and NGO supporters.

If all of this discourse is enacted with an online audience of potential supporters in mind, does that mean we should consider it as purely instrumental or at odds with what leaders of grassroots INGOs really believe? Two findings from the interviews with group leaders give me some confidence that we should not. First, the sort of discourse used to describe recipients and rationales on websites was very similar to what I heard in the interviews. Second, the imagined supporters to whom the websites are addressed are not so very different from the volunteers themselves. For four of the five case study organizations, practically all of the donors were personally known to the board members. Financial and volunteer support came from personal networks: family members, friends, colleagues, or network members at one further remove (colleagues of family members, etc.). These supporters, and not aid experts or major donors, seem like the most likely intended audience for the websites.

We expect that as expressive private aid organizations, grassroots INGOs will work in different locations and on different projects than professionalized aid agencies. An overview of the destinations and projects of the US Agency for International Development (USAID) provides a useful point of departure. I use USAID as a comparison for two reasons. Because USAID is a donor agency—many of its programs are executed through contracts with NGOs—it allows us to see priorities from the top of the aid chain rather than through one specialized contractor. Second, it allows us to see what priorities emerge when an agency must balance scientific expertise with national interest as defined by bureaucrats and politicians. Seeing how grassroots INGO aid differs from official development assistance (ODA) is especially important in an era of public spending cuts, when reductions in ODA are likely to be justified with claims about citizen initiative filling the gaps.

Project Destinations

Tables 2 and 3 show the most common destination regions and countries for grassroots INGOs, while table 4 shows top recipients of USAID economic assistance. Africa is the region most served by grassroots INGOs; more than half of grassroots INGOs studied have at least one project there, while roughly one in three works in Asia and one in four in Latin America.[6] The 15 percent of grassroots INGOs that work in the Caribbean are almost all based in Haiti or the Dominican Republic. Groups working in Europe are mostly in Balkan countries, and the most common Middle Eastern destination is the Palestinian territories.

India is the number one country destination for grassroots INGOs—14 percent of organizations have a project there. The next

TABLE 2. Destination Regions

Percent of organizations with a project in each region

Africa	52%
Asia/Pacific	32%
Latin America (excluding Caribbean)	26%
Caribbean	15%
Middle East/North Africa	7%
Europe/Eurasia	4%

Source: Grassroots INGO websites

TABLE 3. Destination Countries

Percent of organizations with a project in each country

India	14%
Kenya	12%
Haiti	11%
Peru	8%
Mexico	7%
China	7%
Ghana	7%
Uganda	7%
Vietnam	6%
Nepal	5%
Nigeria	5%
Sierra Leone	5%
Guatemala	5%
South Africa	5%
Democratic Republic of Congo	4%
Rwanda	4%
Nicaragua	4%
Indonesia	4%
Cambodia	3%
Colombia	3%
Dominican Republic	3%
Liberia	3%

Source: Grassroots INGO websites

TABLE 4. Top 20 Recipients of Official Development Assistance (Nonmilitary) in 2017

Amount of aid in $US millions	
Afghanistan	$1,341
Ethiopia	$939
South Sudan	$906
Jordan	$897
Kenya	$855
Nigeria	$640
Pakistan	$611
Uganda	$602
South Africa	$592
Syria	$588
Tanzania	$567
Mozambique	$480
Zambia	$473
Malawi	$449
Haiti	$447
Indonesia	$426
Yemen	$416
Congo	$406
Iraq	$381
West Bank/Gaza	$375

Source: USAID Foreign Aid Explorer

most common countries, in descending order, are Kenya, Haiti, Peru, and Mexico. Note that the top two (and three more of the top ten) destination countries are English-speaking; 56 percent of all grassroots INGOs are working in at least one Anglophone country. The destinations of organizations in this sample differ markedly from the top recipients of ODA, which reflects the role of national security interests for even nonmilitary aid. The exceptions are Haiti, Kenya, South Africa, Nigeria, Uganda, and Indonesia, which

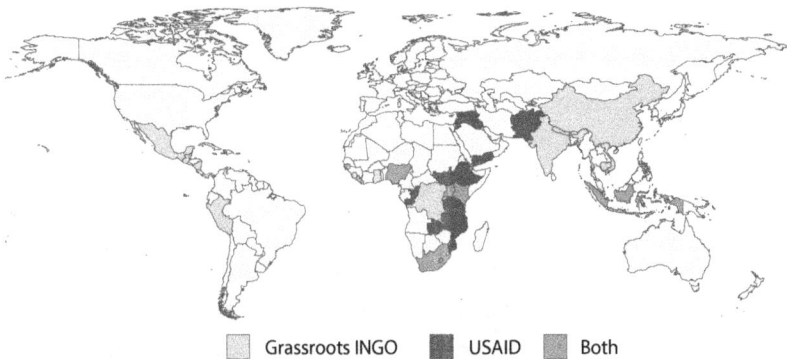

MAP 1. Top destination countries for grassroots INGOs and official development assistance. *Source*: Grassroots INGO websites and USAID Foreign Aid Explorer.

are top locations for grassroots INGOs and were among the top twenty recipients of economic assistance from the US government in 2017, as shown on the map.[7]

How do grassroots INGOs describe their destinations and their reasons for working there? Despite the historical trajectories that shape Americans' interactions with the Global South and that affect patterns of development, grassroots INGOs have surprisingly little to say on their websites about the context of where they work. Only 19 percent of websites offer any historical, economic, or ecological description of the countries where they operate. Of these, only four organizations make any mention of colonial-era history or colonialism itself. This is especially notable given the high percentage of these that operate in Africa, where colonial rule is still in living memory. What websites instead tend to emphasize are relationships that emerge from the founders' previous travel, volunteerism, or work. The following are typical narratives:

During a visit to the majestic Victoria Falls in Zimbabwe in 1998, Janice was rummaging through a nearby gift shop when she came upon a photo album made from unusual, textural paper that was obviously handmade by a local craftsperson. . . . Janice soon located the small pioneering group of papermakers creating unique African style handmade papers. She set up Eco-Africa Papercraft, a social enterprise that would provide skills training and crafting work to hundreds of local women from the impoverished township of Chitungwiza. (Eco Africa Social Ventures)

Women Work Together began in 2007 when Dr. Tracy Ehlers, Associate Professor of Anthropology at the University of Denver, spent a month in San Pedro, Sacatepéquez, Guatemala. . . . Although she'd visited many times from 1977–1996, in 2007 she had not been there for ten years. Her current connection to the town is very strong because, as a graduate student, she lived with the family of the town's current mayor, Dr. Marco Antonio Orozco. . . . At his invitation, they began a collaboration aimed at strengthening women's networks through participatory workshops. (Women Work Together)

The first narrative in particular might be read to hint at the serendipitous quality of global ties. But analyzing these narratives in the aggregate points to just the opposite—the underlying structure of existing connections between the United States and other countries. These narratives suggest that grassroots INGO formation is path dependent on existing global connections between the United States and the rest of the world. Five organizations out of 150 were founded by former Peace Corps volunteers. The disproportionate prevalence of English-speaking countries and greater prevalence of developing countries where American tourists are likely to travel—China and Kenya, over, perhaps, Burundi—are also evidence that Americans having prior opportunities to personally forge links to foreign countries is an important precondition for founding grassroots INGOs.

An equally common founding narrative involves grassroots INGOs emerging from immigration. Four organizations out of 150 were started by the parents of children adopted from India, China, or Ethiopia. One-third of grassroots INGOs in this sample were founded by first- or second-generation immigrants. The websites revealed that these immigrants were most likely to come from Asia or Africa, and most were individuals who had earned a college degree and had reached middle age and middle-class status. Among the founders of organizations in this sample were attorneys, doctors, professors, IT workers, and accountants. While some immigrants partnered with co-ethnics, more commonly the other members of their board were recruited from work or religious congregations and were native-born Americans. It is also worth noting that these immigrants are not representative in their place of descent of the general population of immigrants in the United States. In 2010, nearly 30 percent of immigrants in the United States hailed from Mexico, and just over 50 percent hailed from Latin America generally. Why do Asian and African immigrants seem to disproportionately start grassroots INGOs? It may be because Latin American immigrants interested in providing assistance to their native countries prefer direct remittances or hometown associations. The reason may also be the relationship between education and the organizational form. Grassroots INGOs are typically started by individuals with a bachelor's degree or higher; 13 percent of immigrants from Latin America hold a bachelor's degree or higher, compared with 40 percent or more for immigrants from other regions.[8] Immigrants with less education and lower English fluency might find it difficult to complete the legal maneuvers to register a nonprofit organization.

Project Sectors

The projects of grassroots INGOs run the gamut from capacity building to animal husbandry, but nearly all operate at the level of the community or some smaller unit. They are distinct from projects operated by USAID or multilateral agencies like the World Bank in that they steer clear of infrastructure or industrial development. Like mainstream NGOs, grassroots INGOs target their interventions at the level of the towns or villages, schools, cooperatives, families, or individuals. Table 5 gives a breakdown of the percentages of grassroots INGOs working in the various project sectors.

Education is the dominant area in which these groups work. The majority of organizations support either specific schools or particular students through scholarships. Activate Tanzania, Wellsprings of Hope, and other organizations directly operate schools, while others make cash or in-kind donations to schools run by other organizations. Gifts of books, computers, or other supplies for students are common. Informal educational programs for adults also fall under this category, but more often, programs directed to adults have to do with small business training, Bible courses, or the type of general capacity-building projects commonly seen among mainstream NGOs.[9] The financial dependence of these education projects on grassroots INGOs varies. Some schools, like the one operated by Activate Tanzania, would need to close its doors if the organization ended its support. In other cases,

TABLE 5. Project Sectors

Percent of organizations with a project in each sector	
Education	65%
Medical clinic or supplies	36%
Small business	25%
Clean water	24%
Food provision	19%
English teaching	16%
Orphanage	16%
Christian ministry	15%
Agriculture	14%
Visiting medical teams	12%
Disaster relief	9%
Preservation of cultural heritage	9%
Research	7%
Capacity building	7%
Cultural exchange	7%
Public advocacy	7%
Microcredit	6%
Sports	5%
Family planning	5%
Housing provision	5%
Animal husbandry	4%
Democracy building	3%

Source: Grassroots INGO websites

the consequences would be less dire. The grassroots INGO improves the programs or facilities of the schools or makes attendance possible for very poor students, but other private support or public allocations keep the doors open.

Medical projects are also popular among grassroots INGOs. Over one-third of groups ship supplies or money to medical clinics in the receiving countries. Twelve percent of groups coordinate visits by doctors, nurses, or other specialists to foreign countries.

These visits are typically of several weeks' duration, and often they focus on "in-and-out" procedures like cleft palate surgery that do not require patients to receive ongoing treatment. Some organizations, like the Rwanda Ultrasound Initiative, concentrate on using American personnel to train local medical providers. But training providers rather than treating patients requires coordination with local medical systems, which often means contending with a Ministry of Health. More often, American medical personnel team up with one clinic—private ones, such as those run by missionaries, are popular—and treat patients for several weeks. The clinics then repeat the process with a new visiting team the next year.

Small business projects fall third on the list of most common grassroots INGO projects. Indego Africa provides one example of such projects: women producing handicrafts that are sold to American consumers at fair trade–like prices.[10] This kind of project is popular among the 25 percent of organizations that describe small business programs on their websites. Café Feminino is one of several grassroots INGOs that works with cooperatives to transform subsistence farmers into agricultural businesspeople. Projects to nurture entrepreneurship are also common. Several grassroots INGOs also provide business training programs or mentoring partnerships.

Providing food and clean water are also common activities. Clean water projects also suggest particular interventions: wells. Roughly a quarter of grassroots INGOs provide potable water by digging wells or installing pumps, or else providing funding to other organizations that do this work. These projects are particularly popular in sub-Saharan Africa, Haiti, and India. Projects to directly provide food sometimes occur in the context of disaster relief, but other groups offer "feeding" programs to vulnerable children, or to the chronically poor. (Gifts of food to the poor at

Eid-al-fitr are a common project of Muslim grassroots INGOs.) It is worth noting that projects to directly provide food (19%) are more common than agriculture projects (14%).

The high religiosity of Americans is reflected in the prevalence of Christian ministry activities by grassroots INGOs. Note that under US tax law, nonprofits whose aims are primarily religious are not obligated to register with the government. The organizations in this sample have chosen to identify themselves mainly as international relief, development, or human rights organizations, and yet a full 15 percent also engage in activities that include training pastors, constructing church buildings, evangelizing, and teaching Bible studies. Grassroots INGOs with Catholic and especially evangelical Protestant ties were more likely than mainline Protestant groups to describe ministry activities.

Several project sectors at the bottom of the list are worth a special note. Microcredit, one of the major trends in international development, is practiced by only 6 percent of grassroots INGOs. This is likely because these programs demand considerable financial capital and organizational sophistication. A number of the groups that support microcredit programs do so in partnership with larger organizations. Capacity-building programs are also quite rare, especially compared with the ubiquity of programs for "capacity building" and "empowerment" discussed in the development literature.[11] The political functions of NGOs have long been theorized as one of their essential features.[12] But grassroots INGOs mainly avoid politics in their projects. Only 7 percent engage in public advocacy, and a mere 3 percent work in democracy building.

While USAID categorizes its projects in a different way, we can see that its spending is shaped by humanitarian and political crises. The sectors that are prioritized in economic assistance are

TABLE 6. Top Sectors for Official Development
Assistance (Nonmilitary) in 2017

Amount of aid in $US millions

Emergency response	$6,682
HIV/AIDS	$6,444
Government and civil society	$3,296
Operating expenses	$2,292
Basic health	$2,177
Unallocated/unspecified	$1,699
General environmental protection	$1,366
Agriculture	$1,308
Conflict, peace, and security	$1,250
Basic education	$1,244
Others	$5,508

Source: USAID Foreign Aid Explorer

emergency response, HIV/AIDS, and government/civil society (see
table 6). The United States differs from other donors to the
Organisation for Economic Cooperation and Development (OECD)
in that it does not have special ties to former colonies, but in most
respects its aid giving is similar. Statistics from the OECD show that
the primary sectors for bilateral aid in 2017 were humanitarian assistance ($28 billion), government and civil society ($20 billion), transportation and storage ($17 billion). Health programs were allocated
$12 billion, and population and reproductive health programs, $9.4
billion.[13] Some of the programs funded by USAID will eventually
trickle down to small-scale projects such as building schools or equip-
ping clinics. But the work done by grassroots INGOs favors education
and direct provision of water, food, and medical supplies in development rather than relief contexts, while USAID programs focus on
humanitarian relief, government and civil society, and environmental protection sectors largely neglected by grassroots INGOs.

Roles for US Supporters

Half of the organizations in this sample generated less than $25,000 in annual revenue, so individual supporters are critical for donations and volunteer labor. Prospective supporters are the audience of the websites analyzed here, and their roles in grassroots INGOs are on display in two ways on websites. The first is through depictions of existing volunteer support—particularly testimonials from donors and accounts of volunteer trips. "News" or blog sections of websites often give accounts of fundraisers or events that offer a window into existing supporter roles. The more explicit way we learn what supporters can do is through the requests made on websites. Nearly every site has a page labeled "Donate," "How You Can Help," or similar, with one or more of the tasks given in table 7.

Requests for cash donations are ubiquitous and are absent mostly from organizations that operate international exchange programs where volunteers pay fees rather than make open-ended donations. Supporters are encouraged to increase the audience for the organization by "liking" a Facebook page or following on Twitter. Child sponsorships are a more narrowly tailored sort of donation wherein a supporter offers a recurring monthly donation to support the school fees or maintenance of an individual child. Under these arrangements—popularized by Save the Children in the 1980s—US supporters typically receive a photograph and capsule biography of their sponsored child. In acknowledgment of the assistance they receive, sponsored children (typically with the assistance of teachers or NGO staff) write letters once or twice a year to their American sponsors. This fundraising tactic became broadly used by larger NGOs beginning in the 1980s because it

TABLE 7. Roles for US Supporters

Percent of organizations offering each role

Donate money	91%
Follow on social media	43%
Volunteer abroad	35%
Volunteer in US	33%
Donate goods	25%
Sponsor child	13%
Pray	13%

Source: Grassroots INGO websites

increased donations by putting a (young, typically dark-skinned) face on complex and overwhelming development issues.[14] In the wake of the negative publicity that came from a 1998 *Chicago Tribune* report on child sponsorship programs, most NGOs that use child sponsorship note specifically on the website whether all of sponsors' funds go directly to a child or whether a share will be used for general operating expenses. Thirteen percent of grassroots INGOs in this sample use this funding model, and most of them boast that 100 percent of a donation goes directly to the sponsored child.

Volunteer labor is the third thing that supporters can provide. Approximately three out of ten organizations solicit volunteer work in the United States. (This is only organizations that *publicly solicit* volunteers on their website; virtually all of these groups use some volunteer labor for their administration in the United States) Because many grassroots INGOs are so small, it is not unusual for organizations to solicit volunteers for basic administrative tasks such as handling mailings or website maintenance. Experts in grant-writing or fundraising are in high demand.[15] Organizations' leaders often turn to their family members to support their work. Of the 150 websites here, 41 listed family members working together on the board of directors or in other volunteer roles. Bigger-budget, more established grassroots INGOs look more like other formalized nonprofit organizations: board members are recruited on the basis of their professional expertise or fundraising capacity, and paid staff (often part-time) are employed for administrative support.

The place of volunteers in the delivery of aid itself is one of the critical differences between grassroots and mainstream INGOs. Oxfam, CARE, and their peers—like government aid agencies— only employ trained staff, typically with relevant university degrees and years of experience in the US office, to carry out the projects themselves in the receiving communities. But over one-third of the grassroots INGOs here publicly recruit volunteers for work abroad. In most cases, these are for short-term visits of a few weeks to a few months. Some organizations recruit volunteers with very specific technical skills (especially in medicine or engineering), but more commonly volunteers sign up for low-skill projects. Often the projects these volunteers engage in, such as landscaping or construction of community buildings, draw on the unskilled manual labor that is abundant in the receiving community. As I discuss in chapter 3, the logic underlying these projects is not based on efficiency or cost effectiveness, but on cultivating relationships between volunteers and the host communities.

A quarter of organizations request in-kind donations. In ten out of thirty-eight cases, the request is for goods that will be used in the United States (for example, office supplies or art and other items that can be auctioned at a fundraiser). In seven cases the request for goods came following a natural disaster. But often the goods solicited are first aid supplies, small gifts for children like pencils or toys, or fabric that can be used in craft workshops. These items are typically packed into suitcases and brought as checked luggage with visiting volunteers. Donations of goods thus support domestic administration, fundraising, project implementation, and relations with people (especially children) in the receiving communities.

The role of religion in grassroots INGOs is seen in another thing that the organizations ask of their supporters: prayer. Thirteen percent of grassroots INGOs ask supporters to pray for their work. The Circle of Hope website cites inspiration from an evangelical missionary in forming a "24 hour prayer team" to pray "throughout the day and the night for the ministry and vision Jesus has given us for healing in Africa." Another group asked supporters "to be with us in prayer regarding fundraising and finances" (7 Day Hero). Others ask for prayers for the safety of traveling volunteers.

Partner Organizations

Grassroots INGOs collaborate with a variety of other organizations to raise money and to carry out their work. While websites offer incomplete accounts of the depth and dynamics of these partnerships, they provide some indications about the sort of organizations with whom grassroots INGOs share an orbit. In short, these findings give further evidence that the networks in which grassroots INGOs are embedded are far different from the professional aid field that mainstream NGOs inhabit.

In the countries in which they work, grassroots INGOs frequently collaborate with other international NGOs (39%) or with host-country NGOs (32%)—known in some regions as community-based organizations (CBOs)—to carry out their projects (see table 8). In some cases, the grassroots INGO exists essentially to raise funds for programs run entirely by CBOs—this is a particularly

TABLE 8. Partner Organizations

Percent of organizations listing each type of partner

INGO	39%
NGO based in aid-receiving country/CBO	32%
Religious congregation in US	28%
Religious congregation in aid-receiving community	27%
Business donor	26%
Artists or arts organizations	25%
Government in receiving country (any level)	24%
US university	22%
Rotary club	15%
US school	15%
Diaspora organization	12%
US government (any level)	11%
International chapter/affiliate	9%
Business partner	9%
Foundation donor	8%
Peace Corps	7%
Other US affiliate/chapter	5%
Cooperative	4%
Retail partner	3%

Source: Grassroots INGO websites

common relationship with schools and orphanages. Other sorts of contracting and collaborative relationships are possible, and nearly half of all organizations mention a partnership with another NGO on their website. Mentions of major INGOs like the International Rescue Committee and CARE are very rare, and virtually no grassroots INGOs mention a relationship with bilateral or multilateral aid agencies. Twenty-four percent of grassroots INGOs discuss a relationship with some agency or level of the receiving-country government. These relationships can be as superficial as photo ops with government ministers, as bureaucratic as receiving official approval to work in the country, or as substantial as developing a curriculum module for local doctors in collaboration with the Ministry of Health. Most commonly, the relationship is with a local government body rather than the national government—these higher-level bodies typically limit themselves to partnerships with larger private, bilateral, or multilateral aid agencies.

Of other partners in the aid-receiving country, religious congregations are most common. As I describe in chapter 7, partnering with a religious congregation offers grassroots INGOs common languages and practices that make it easier to reach beneficiaries. Three of the case study groups—Activate Tanzania, Wellsprings of Hope, and For Kenya's Tomorrow—employed such partnerships. In the case of the latter two organizations, the pastors of the congregations became the local "brokers" for the grassroots INGOs' work. Seven percent of organizations work with former or active Peace Corps volunteers; these individuals typically contribute country-specific expertise, or are partners in implementing projects. Other common local partners include artisan or agricultural cooperatives.

At home, grassroots INGOs most often collaborate with religious congregations and businesses. (Chapter 7 describes in greater depth the way that grassroots INGOs use religious congregations to generate volunteers, cash, and supplies.) The most common role for businesses is offering cash or in-kind donations; a quarter of grassroots INGOs list this kind of relationship. Almost one in ten have some other sort of partnership with a business, often involving volunteer recruitment or mentoring programs. A small number of grassroots INGOs partner with retail businesses to sell goods produced by the groups' beneficiaries. The goods for sale are often cottage-industry products like jewelry, baskets, or paper crafts; high-end coffee is another popular item. The ability of grassroots INGOs to have their own online shops is partially obviating the need for these sort of brick-and-mortar retail partnerships. Indego Africa started by seeking out museum gift shops, but today the majority of its sales are either through its online store or via contracts with retailers like Tom's Shoes.

Artists or arts organizations are common partners, but typically the art is being used as a fundraising tool. The sale of CDs, paintings, and photographs is a common fundraising technique. Music or dance groups—especially those with ties to the aid-receiving country—perform at fundraising events. Arts occasionally are the substance of the grassroots INGO's project; Fundacion ALMA sees arts as integral to development, describing its mission as to "strengthen communities and promote peace through music and arts education." A few grassroots INGOs host foreign artists and exhibitions.

Other partner organizations provide volunteers, knowledge resources, or public platforms for grassroots INGOs. Schools, universities, diaspora organizations, and Rotary Clubs fit this profile. These organizations are critical to the public influence of grassroots INGOs in the United States, because they are channels by which the latter convey ideas about development and the people who receive it. School partnerships often involve pen-pal relationships or video chats between American children and partners abroad; university partnerships can involve research projects (often the researcher plays a critical role in the grassroots INGO) or fundraising from student groups. A handful (10%) of grassroots INGOs are members of a federation and have chapters or affiliates elsewhere in the United States or abroad.

Just over 11 percent of groups discuss a relationship with elected officials or agencies of municipal, state, or federal government in the United States. As with foreign governments, sometimes the connections mentioned on websites are cameo appearances by an ambassador or a member of Congress thanking the grassroots INGO for its efforts. More substantial relationships take one of two forms. One is a partnership or exchange program between municipalities in the United States and a country in the global South. The second is an advocacy relationship vis-à-vis the US government, where the grassroots INGO lobbies the government for political action on behalf of some constituency in the Global South. But for most groups, engagement with government agencies in the United States is limited to completing their annual tax-exempt online form for the IRS.

Aid Recipients

Grassroots INGOs' websites depict the status designations and personal qualities of the people who receive aid. Some projects, like providing clean water, have benefits for the community at large, so websites offer little description of particular recipients. But many organizations target specific status groups and are explicit about this on their websites. The second sentence of Pathways/Africa's website reads, "Pathways/Africa is a U.S.-based nonprofit organization committed to investing in the future of African children."

According to the organizations' websites, children and youth are the group most frequently targeted, with almost six in ten organizations describing a project for their benefit. A bit more than half of the organizations that targeted children or youth worked specifically for the benefit of orphans, most often by running orphanages, offering scholarships, or providing material support

TABLE 9. Status Designations of Aid Recipients

Percent of organizations targeting each recipient category

Children/youth	60%
Women	36%
Orphans	32%
Men	11%

Source: Grassroots INGO websites

for orphans' caregivers. As shown in table 9, women were designated as recipients by 36 percent of organizations, compared with only 11 percent of organizations naming male recipients.

The high visibility of children and the near invisibility of men persist in the images that grassroots INGOs use on their websites. Of images on the organization's home page (i.e., the first page of the site), children appeared in nearly half the images (46%); photographs of women appeared about half as often as children (26%). American volunteers were equally likely to be featured in pictures on the homepage (12%) as were local men.

How were these aid recipients depicted? Nearly half of all organizations describe them as living in deprived conditions, and a common discursive tactic on websites is to include a short biography tracing how the recipient's life has been changed through her contact with the grassroots INGO—or what her hopes for the future are, pending continuing support from the organization. Even though children, youth, and women are the most common recipients of assistance, personal narratives feature them disproportionately, in twenty-six out of twenty-nine cases where the stories of individuals living in deprivation are told. This supports the suggestion that these groups are imagined as the most broadly legitimate recipients of aid. Although *texts* describing recipients' suffering were common, the *images* on homepages far more often depicted recipients smiling (21%) than visibly suffering (6%).

There are rare references on websites to theft by an employee or to prostitution or drug and alcohol abuse by people in recipient communities. On websites that describe such blameworthy behavior by recipients (5%), the story is usually tied to a description of deprived conditions. A text from the Families in Vietnam webpage is typical of such references in that it also describes mitigating circumstances (desperation, hopelessness), and the possibility for change, with the organization's help: "Social destruction begins to occur in these families when the hopelessness of continuing starts to consume them and they fall victim to the many trappings of the truly desperate and despondent that must provide for their children to eat: prostitution, drug-use and selling, and so on. We at FIV put ourselves, often literally, between the families and these deceptive, destructive and temporary trappings and guide them to better choices, with your sponsorship."

The more typical portrayal on grassroots INGO websites is of morally worthy recipients in difficult conditions beyond their control. Table 10 gives percentages of texts that describe recipients using language of work ethic (23%), future ambition (17%) and kindness or hospitality (17%). Orphans and the disabled are those who are usually described as "vulnerable," but the descriptor is also applied to minority ethnic groups or communities at large in the wake of wars or disaster (19%). This term designates a group as deserving of aid by virtue of its special status. In contrast, other texts make claims for recipients on the grounds that humans everywhere are essentially the same (14%). This discourse about shared humanity speaks to common human nature and desires. A volunteer for an education organization in Uganda wrote on the

TABLE 10. Qualitative Descriptions of Aid Recipients

Percent of organizations using each description	
Living in deprived conditions	43%
Hardworking	23%
Vulnerable	19%
Has future ambitions	17%
Kind, good, or hospitable	17%
Shared humanity	14%

Source: Grassroots INGO websites

group's website, "The stories were compelling, but what shone out was their humanness. They were eager to forgive, eager to let go of the past and look towards the future, eager to love"(Friends of UNIFAT). In sum, women and especially children are the most common recipients of grassroots INGOs' aid. These people are most often described as worthy recipients and kind hosts; as deprived, but with the capacity for transformation.

Aid Rationales

Grassroots INGOs often go further in their discourse than describing the worthiness of recipients, to offering broader rationales for Americans to intervene in a foreign community. Some rationales rely on references to international agencies like the World Health Organization, to establish that an issue or type of intervention is important. Other texts make abstract claims based on principles of human rights, gender equality, or justice. But as shown in table 11, the most common rationale, used by over one-third of groups, relies on the implicit claim that human suffering demands a response, and the texts themselves focus on explaining the source of the suffering. For example: "For children living in poverty, every

TABLE 11. Rationales

Percent of organizations invoking each rationale	
Suffering	35%
God's purposes	26%
Following international authority	18%
Human rights	15%
Political strife	13%
Justice	12%
War	12%
Epidemic disease	10%
Gender inequality	9%
Natural disaster	7%
Oppression by outside groups	7%

Source: Grassroots INGO websites

day is filled with challenges, missed opportunities, and broken dreams. The dividing line between rich and poor is education. Many children living in poor countries have no choices regarding education; there are no schools. The Village School Foundation believes children should not be neglected and deserve to be educated." The organization goes on to explain how their work will alleviate the suffering: "The Rural Schools program builds new schools in areas where access for children is difficult or where schools do not exist. Access to education gives children the opportunity to learn, develop skills, and build confidence—helping them support themselves and their families." (Village School Foundation) Other rationales are more specific and pragmatic, emphasizing extraordinary events that necessitate aid: war (12%), epidemic (10%), natural disaster (7%), and other sorts of political conflict (13%).

The second most common rationales, used by 26% of organizations, are religious. The rationales coded here as "God's purposes" take several specific forms: they describe projects as material demonstrations of God's love or as obedience to what volunteers understand as God's will or a "calling" to take particular action. The "calling" variation of this rationale most often comes from evangelical groups, but a Catholic group described being inspired by Mary to combine a religious pilgrimage with a housing-repair volunteer project: "Our Lady put it strongly in Jeff's heart that this project was about more than just roofs. It was about the priceless gift of hope. . . . Thus, at our Lady's behest, St. David's hosted forty-two Americans of amazingly diverse backgrounds on this working pilgrimage in order to fan the embers of hope into a flame in the little Bosnian town of Boderiste" (St. David's Relief).

Appeals to abstract principles of human rights or justice (15% and 13%, respectively) are not half as common as appeals to relieve suffering. In some cases, human rights are described in political terms and are associated with rights to autonomy. But in other cases, access to basic services is described as a human right. Africa in Mind writes, "Literacy becomes an absolute tool for personal empowerment and a means for social and human development. It is a human right!" Plumbers, too, are agents for human rights, according to the Plumbers Without Borders website: "Safe water and sanitation are human rights!"

. . .

Most grassroots INGOs do not issue annual reports or provide data on their programs to intermediary organizations. These groups' websites provide the best data available to date on their foreign locations, projects, recipients, networks, and roles for private supporters. We have seen that grassroots INGOs differ from official development assistance in their destinations, which are shaped less by national interest than by linguistic, religious, and migratory affinities. Programs to provide education, medical supplies and personnel, small business training, and clean water are most popular. Websites must not be understood as a perfect audit of grassroots INGO practices, but these texts point to children and women as the most common aid recipients. Texts depict recipients of aid as individuals in difficult circumstances, but with a work ethic and ambitions for the future.

Some grassroots INGOs cite abstract rationales of justice or human rights for their work. But in further evidence of their distinction from professionalized aid organizations, they less often invoke the authority of local government officials or scientific experts than divine authority: God's love or God's calling were used as a rationale for work by a quarter of groups. Most often, though, grassroots INGOs rely on claims that humans are suffering and that others have a responsibility to respond.

American supporters are asked to help by donating money, goods, or time (either in the United States or in the aid-receiving country). Volunteer service ranges from the typical nonprofit roles of envelope stuffing and grant writing to performing surgeries and mentoring businesswomen. Grassroots INGOs also ask supporters to pray for them or to increase their visibility by following them on social media. Besides individual supporters, grassroots INGOs partner with international and local NGOs, government agencies, foundations, religious congregations, Rotary Clubs, diaspora groups, and schools.

We can draw at least two conclusions about the contributions of grassroots INGOs to relief and development in the Global South from this analysis. First, private giving via grassroots INGOs does not necessarily respond to the areas of greatest need or the regions that have been identified as development priorities by the US government. At a moment when threats to foreign aid are regularly discussed, even dramatic increases in giving to grassroots INGOs could not substitute for the sort of work carried out with official development assistance.

Second, although most grassroots INGOs are nominally doing development work rather than humanitarian relief, their projects mainly involve direct provision of scholarships, goods, or services. Other than projects that support public schools, grassroots INGOs mainly choose work that allows them to avoid politics or collaboration with government. This work either allows the organization to stand in for the family or state or to provide aid recipients with new skills that should allow them to flourish. As I show in the next two chapters, these approaches to aid—especially the role of American volunteers—diverges from the contemporary professional approach to aid, and in many ways harkens to the approaches of the past.

3   *Amateurs without Borders*

A Role for Everyday Citizens in Development Aid

In development economist Angus Deaton's book *The Great Escape* there is a telling disjuncture between the preface and the chapters that follow. In the preface, Deaton relays the story of his father, Leslie Harold, who was born in 1918 in an English coal-mining town. Leslie escaped the mines to train with a British commando unit in World War II, but because of a bout with tuberculosis was spared participation in a disastrous 1942 raid on occupied Norway. After leaving the army he married a Scottish girl and studied at night to become a civil engineer; the couple scrimped and saved to leave grimy Edinburgh for the countryside, where Leslie nurtured young Angus to a scholarship at a prestigious secondary school. From there, the younger Deaton went on to Cambridge and eventually, to Princeton, where he now holds an endowed chair and was awarded the Nobel Memorial Prize for his work in development economics.

Deaton uses the story of his family's generational mobility to illustrate the magnificent gains in health and wealth enjoyed by much of the world's population starting in the late eighteenth century. He acknowledges that humankind's "great escape" from poverty has left more than a billion people behind, and in the last section of the book he addresses the possibilities of development aid to eliminate poverty in less-developed countries. His argument is that aid fails because it undermines the democratic institutions that foster long-term development. What is needed instead, according to Deaton, are technological advances—a malaria vaccine, for instance—fairer deals in international trade negotiations, technical advice, and more generous migration policies. He says that well-meaning Americans would do best to advocate these solutions rather than volunteering their own time and money or lobbying wealthy countries to increase their foreign aid.[1]

The beginning and the ending of Deaton's book exemplify opposing narratives about development. The latter is an *expert narrative*. Deaton differs from his colleagues on some particulars, but he represents basic points of consensus among social scientific experts on development. The expert narrative of development embraces the human capabilities approach pioneered by Amartya Sen, which identifies well-being in health, education, and democratic participation as both the *ends* and *means* of development.[2] It emphasizes technical expertise and the legal, economic, and political institutions that create the infrastructure for growth and keep the state accountable to citizens.[3] From this perspective, aid efforts must complement rather than supplant the development of local capacity.

Yet the themes that emerge from the Deaton family's rise from poverty are good luck (a case of tuberculosis at the right moment), hard work (night school to achieve professional qualification), and a "hand up" from a charitable benefactor (Angus Deaton's scholarship to a private school). Change a few of the geographic particulars and we can easily imagine this family as a success story on a grassroots INGO's website. The paradox in Deaton's presentation is that while he uses the expert narrative of development as a prescription, he recognizes the emotional power of the popular narrative of development illustrated by his family's rags-to-riches story.

Stories like Deaton's still hold their appeal for citizens of developed countries. While the definitions of development and prescriptions of how to achieve it have evolved, everyday citizens are still moved by the ideas of a "hand up" and individual transformation. These stories of individual socioeconomic mobility aided by charitable benefactors are often the sort of blueprints that Americans bring with them when they get involved in grassroots INGOs. Development becomes a matter of transforming countries one Deaton at a time.

In this chapter I trace how the definition of development that guides mainstream aid agencies has become more complex and elusive, thereby excluding well-meaning amateurs from participating in aid work. But by the end of the twentieth century, countervailing changes had increased the ways that Americans could make contact with people in developing countries. The affordances of globalization allow amateurs to create organizations where they can do things that are impossible through mainstream aid organizations. I draw on the case study interviews and website texts to show that grassroots INGOs allow amateurs three crucial things: the chance to work directly with beneficiaries, the opportunity to share their vocational skills, and a way to "pass on" the lessons learned from their and their families' stories of socioeconomic mobility.

Transformation of the Definition of Development and the Role of NGOs

Susan Cotts Watkins and her colleagues have argued that the goals of international development have become broader and vaguer. A

1958 article in the *Economist* described the goals of American private development aid in that era: "The things aimed at are those which, to an American eye, appear most needed—health and clean water, plentiful crops, houses with tight roofs."[4] But as Watkins and her colleagues note, the goals of development shifted. By 1991, the journal *World Development* defined development as "improving standards of living, and the human condition generally, by examining potential solutions to problems such as: poverty, unemployment, malnutrition, disease, illiteracy, lack of shelter, environmental degradation, inadequate scientific and technological resources, trade and payments imbalances, international debt, gender and ethnic discrimination, violation of human rights, militarism and civil conflict, and lack of popular participation in economic and political life."[5] To achieve such broad goals required more radical transformations in individual subjectivities and social organization. Development aid increasingly emphasized the process of engaging beneficiaries, making participation both the means and ends of development.[6]

What do NGOs actually do, day to day, to bring about these transformations? Mainly, they talk. Watkins and colleagues find that NGO work increasingly consists of meetings and trainings. Meetings bring together stakeholders, assess needs, create plans, and evaluate progress. Trainings are the technology by which change is meant to happen. They describe trainings that "teach people to embrace democracy, practice safe sex to prevent AIDS, protect forests, reduce gender-based violence, or otherwise transform their lives. Like funding, talk cascades downward. Donors talk with elite brokers at international meetings and when they visit NGO offices in the capital. The elite brokers pass the talk on to their subcontractors, and so on down the line. Brokers at the smaller NGOs then deploy the talking technology to train the volunteers whose job it is to talk to the members of their community about the importance of participation and empowerment for their future prosperity."[7] All of this talk is distant from the 1950s projects of digging wells, raising crops, and building houses.

David Korten elaborates this evolution of NGO work in his well-known "four generations" typology of NGO aid. Korten observed in the NGOs he encountered in Asia a progressive transformation of development strategies that moved in four stages from addressing *symptoms* of poverty to *causes*. Each stage is marked by distinctive projects, roles for NGOs, and scope for action.

First-generation approaches focus on *relief and welfare*; the role of the NGO is to ensure that people's immediate needs are met. This strategy characterized the approach of nascent international NGOs that provided relief after the world wars in Europe. In this generation of aid, the level of intervention is typically the individual or the family. Second-generation strategies of *community development* view inertia as the impediment to development, and so NGOs catalyze people into identifying their own problems and organizing solutions. The aim is to build self-reliance so that development will continue after the NGOs' involvement has ended. Importantly, this strategy engages not just individuals but larger-level collectivities—typically neighborhoods or villages. It assumes that collective capacity, while slow to build, is needed for further development. Third-generation strategies aim to reform institutions and policies that impede development—the goal is to create *sustainable systems*. The level of intervention rises again, to the level of the region or the nation, and NGOs' role shifts to providing political leverage or financial or technical assistance to local partners. This strategy demands engagement with politicians and bureaucrats, often over a span of decades. Finally, Korten describes elusive fourth-generation *people's movements* that extend beyond national borders. These are broader social movements, where NGOs act in global networks to fundamentally alter power relations. Korten describes these generations as a macro-history of NGO approaches to development in the twentieth century, but he also argues that individual NGOs tend to evolve from first-generation strategies to more "sophisticated" third-generation ones.[8] His writing on third- and fourth-generation NGOs reflects the view, widely shared at the end of the twentieth century, that good aid builds local capacity and that creating good institutions is a central task of development.[9]

This shift in the role of NGOs was broadly accepted by funders and NGOs themselves, and so the place for well-intentioned amateurs among these groups virtually disappeared. Hiring local staff for substantive roles became a best practice for aid organizations, and the positions left for natives of the United States and other developed countries dwindled and became fiercely competitive. Today, an American looking to work or volunteer full-time in international development faces a selection process designed to weed out all but the most dedicated and qualified candidates. Prospective Peace Corps volunteers must hold a bachelor's degree or equivalent work experience and undergo a months-long application process that includes a written application, in-person interview, fingerprinting, background check, and medical clearance. An entry-level job with an international NGO is rarer still. The Columbia University School of International and Public Affairs advises candidates with a bachelor's degree that these positions "will likely involve administrative support . . . in the U.S. headquarters. Opportunities for international travel and experience are likely to be very limited."

They further advise candidates to gain international experience through Peace Corps service or similar programs before continuing on to a graduate degree, as "a graduate degree is essential to pursue a career in international development."[10]

But as amateurs have been crowded out of official development work, new ways for them to connect with developing countries have emerged. Migration patterns in the latter twentieth century brought millions of immigrants from China, India, and Mexico to the United States. These migrants, unlike their earlier predecessors, settled all over the United States, from burgeoning tech metropolises like Dallas to small Midwestern towns in decline. Nearly seven hundred thousand immigrants came from Haiti, establishing diaspora communities primarily in Florida and New York. Wars also pushed refugees from Sudan and Myanmar into unlikely new homes in the upper Midwest and Rust Belt. International adoption became more common, creating blood ties between American families and China, Russia, Guatemala, Ethiopia, and Vietnam.[11]

Americans can travel to and communicate more cheaply with developing countries than ever before. The price of airline tickets in real dollars decreased dramatically starting in the 1980s, and international travel became affordable for more Americans. In 1960, only two out of ten Americans had ever been on an airplane; in 2015, thirty-two million Americans took international flights.[12] And technology made it possible for people in the United States to maintain these ties to people they encountered when abroad. International phone calls from the United States averaged $7 per minute in the 1970s, while today a call to India costs $0.28 per minute on a landline, and is virtually free on Skype.[13] Mobile phones make it possible to communicate with people in places where landline telephone service was never established. By 2014, nine out of ten people in Asia had a cell phone subscription, as did seven out of ten in Africa.[14] And when people want to send money from place to place, that same cellular technology has made it simple to wire money through services like Western Union and MoneyGram. These services were once anchored in post offices or banks that had landline phones, limiting their combined number of agents to about one hundred fifty thousand in 2001. By 2018 the number of cash transfer agents was nine hundred thousand, allowing people in developing countries to access cash from abroad without an arduous, days-long trip to a regional city.[15]

In sum, two patterns in the late twentieth and early twenty-first century had countervailing effects. The increasing professionalization of international development made it harder for everyday Americans to be involved in mainstream forms of aid. But Americans had opportunities to build ties to developing countries through other means, as migrants arrived, Americans traveled, and people could communicate cheaply across international borders. It was these international connections, as we saw in chapter 1, that laid the groundwork for Americans to establish grassroots international NGOs.

What Can Amateurs Do through Grassroots International NGOs?

Development aid as practiced by conventional actors excludes everyday citizens from doing much but writing checks. The sympathetic American might contribute cash to a large NGO, but her common sense, work experience, and volunteer time are deemed irrelevant and unwelcome. Grassroots INGOs, however, do not confine themselves to expert knowledge. They do not confront development as a "wicked problem" to be attacked systematically through decades of scientific research and bureaucratic lessons learned. In their narrative of development, adequate human knowledge and resources exist; the problem is how to transfer these things across borders from those who have it to those who do not.

What happens when amateurs can become personally involved in aid? Grassroots international NGOs are fundamentally different from other aid channels because they can be supply driven and expressive. That is, they can be driven by the preferences, skills, and ideas of its leaders rather than having to respond to the specific demands of either beneficiaries or big donors. Monika Krause has written about how large NGOs are constantly shifting their projects to align with the tastes of donor agencies—they must judiciously create projects that respond to donors' priorities and that allow them to measure their success.[16] Avoiding the grant and contract economy allows grassroots INGOs to choose the work that appeals to the American volunteers. Free from the constraints of measurement and evaluation that large NGOs face, grassroots INGOs can prioritize the experience that people have in working with the organization, and not merely the quantity or quality of the services provided. These organizations thus provide three kinds of opportunities for well-intentioned amateurs that would be impossible in other aid settings.

Working Directly with Beneficiaries

Grassroots INGOs offer Americans the chance to get their hands dirty. Unlike most aid organizations, these groups welcome international volunteers; recall from chapter 2 that a third of these groups solicited volunteers to go abroad on their websites. Many organizations emphasized that *anyone* could make a difference. A board member of Wellsprings of Hope explained to me that even a volunteer without hard skills was useful: "Everyone has skills, but they're all just different. And there's some skills that come to people's mind . . . you think of construction, medical, education. There's a lot of other skills that are really necessary that you just don't think of." He named "compassion" as such as skill.

The founder of For Kenya's Tomorrow explained that giving Americans the opportunity to volunteer was one of her priorities: "I wanted it to be an open door for people to come and serve." Why bring Americans overseas to do low-skill work? A former volunteer for a housing blitz in Bosnia explained that the experience of solidarity between American workers and local partners was the true reward of the project: "The workweek was a true pilgrimage and a test of faith. We worked through the week in a steady rain. Everybody pitched in and worked as hard as they could go for ten and sometimes twelve hours a day. . . . One thing that made this project so meaningful to the locals and Americans was that the humanitarian aid was given face to face. There was no massive bureaucracy doling out huge amounts of materials. It was a transatlantic barn-raising" (St. David's Relief).

The emotional or spiritual experience of volunteering is essential to these groups' approach. Volunteers describe in their narratives how, they, not just recipients, have been changed by the projects: "I never imagined last September that my life would change as much as it has these last few months. . . . I not only mean physically and mentally, but also a heartstring-pulling and heart-fulfilling change" (Light of the World Charities). An American volunteering at a school in Africa similarly writes, "My own world is much, much bigger now, and richer in every way" (Pathways/Africa).

This is consistent with what Ann Swidler and Susan Cotts Watkins have characterized as the "romance" of AIDS altruism in Africa. They describe both Western altruists and the "brokers" who connect them with beneficiaries as players in a romance, with the former longing to help, and the latter hoping to find income and job prospects. While their use of the term *romance* does not signal an erotic connection between altruists and brokers, Swidler and Watkins very deliberately emphasize the emotional freight of the relationships. They write, "As in a love story, both [Western altruists and African brokers] long for connection, albeit in different ways. They bring to their encounters their own hopes and dreams, and they often suffer disappointment and heartbreak. Sometimes there is an eventual consummation, if not a perfectly happy ending."[17]

For many grassroots INGOs, these emotional experiences and the personal relationships in which they emerge serve as both an *end* and *means* of their work. Trusting personal relationships between Americans and local partners become the means for amateurs to learn about local context and receive feedback on their work. The feedback that local partners provide in the context of friendship substitutes for the knowledge that INGOs accumulate from years of professional experience and the formal processes of assessment carried out by staff. Wellsprings of Hope, for example, relies on the personal relationships between American leaders and Ugandan counterparts to guide the process of project planning. American volunteers have pushed for smaller class sizes and higher instructional quality in the schools, as well as income-generating projects; the Ugandan leaders have pushed for salaries for pastors and the purchase of a truck. Wellsprings does not turn to things like the Sustainable Development Goals or to formal assessment processes to select priorities. Instead, Wellsprings' president explains that ongoing conversations and trust are the keys to adjudicating differences: "It's what enables the ministry to do what they do, the partnership between the US side and the Uganda side, if the trust wasn't there, or violated, naturally things would change." No volunteers, no relationships, no trust, no programs. (In a later chapter I show how this arrangement was nearly the undoing of the organization.) Grassroots INGOs facilitate relationships between Americans and local partners that provide emotional satisfaction and—when all goes well—a functional source of on-the-ground knowledge.

Sharing Vocational Skills

Grassroots INGOs not only allow Americans to work shoulder-to-shoulder with local partners but, more specifically, they also provide chances for Americans in a variety of fields to share their vocational skills. Only a handful of large NGOs such as ACDI/VOCA solicit volunteers with specialized skills for international work. Grassroots INGOs provide a channel for a supply of willing volunteers whose particular skills, interests, or availability do not align with the very small demand from other organizations. Thus, grassroots international NGOs' programs are often designed to allow volunteers to share skills honed in their careers.

This impulse to share skills goes beyond the medical field; doctors are not the only ones without borders. More than fifty aid organizations with similar names are registered with the IRS, including the following:

Engineers Without Borders
Plumbers Without Borders
Sociologists Without Borders
Clergy Beyond Borders
Osteopathy Without Borders
Education Without Borders
Executives Without Borders
Monks Without Borders
Inventors Without Borders
C.I.O.s Without Borders
Professors Beyond Borders

Speakers Without Borders
Business Across Borders
Translators Without Borders
Chefs Without Borders
Radiologists Without Borders
Teachers Without Borders
Astronomers Without Borders
Toxicologists Without Borders
Builders Without Borders
International Healers Without
Borders

Among the case study groups, the possibility of sharing vocational skills was the motivating idea of the Rwanda Ultrasound Initiative: extending training on diagnostic ultrasound from American to Rwandan doctors. One of the founders, Tamara, described her reaction to seeing unused equipment at Rwandan hospitals: "I found these machines, these two beautiful, brand-new machines off in some side room. I would be using that every second of the day, but if they don't know how to use it then it's totally wasted, and it's this amazing technology." This goal of sharing her skills with counterparts abroad was central to Tamara's motivation to engage in aid work.

While some of these groups carry out direct service, others build capacity among workers in developing countries. The opportunity to share work skills with African counterparts was especially appealing to the volunteers of the case study groups I interviewed, including five doctors, two accountants, two pastors, two teachers, a nurse, and a librarian. Wellsprings of Hope leaders explained how their programs expanded from a child-sponsorship program into teacher training and health care after a librarian and a nurse joined the board. For this board member, the opportunity to use her skills in Africa felt providential. Frances said, "Everything in my life had prepared me for that experience . . . in terms of my Christian development, in terms of my professional development, in terms of my interest in traveling. It just seemed like this big confluence of factors. And here I was, setting up a library in a place that desperately needed one, and had the space, and had all these horrible books that had been shipped over there from in the '60s. I don't know where they came from. But I know what to do with that." This volunteer moved from a direct-service capacity—setting up a library—to training the teachers at Wellsprings of Hope's schools in American pedagogical techniques. Like other volunteers I interviewed, Frances describes being able to work with African counterparts as one of the most satisfying parts of her volunteer work.

But does it make sense to transplant American vocational skills into developing-country settings? Frances explains that her efforts to introduce textbooks and interactive learning styles mainly failed. She says, "When I first went, I really was intent on making it right by my standards. And I don't worry about that too much anymore; just plant the seeds, and give ideas. . . . And some of it sticks and some of it maybe won't, but it's okay." The physician volunteers of RUI assured me that medical training was medical training, and they could teach local physicians to use diagnostic ultrasound in the same way that they had learned in the United States. But they also conceded that local doctors found the techniques useful in different ways than doctors in American hospitals, given the types of injuries and illnesses that were common in Rwanda. Local resources also limited the utility of the ultrasound training. Some doctors who received the training were then transferred by the Ministry of Health to district hospitals without ultrasound machines, rendering their new skills useless.

Using Volunteers' Own Lives as a Model for Success

Grassroots international NGOs allow amateurs to "get their hands dirty," to make use of their vocational skills abroad, and to use their own stories of economic mobility—the Deaton-esque success story—as blueprints for development. In creating projects and interacting with aid recipients, volunteers portray hard work in school and in business as viable paths to success even in poor countries. The founder of Indego Africa explained that he looked to his grandmother's biography in creating a women's microenterprise project in Rwanda.

> [T]here was a narrative from my family history that was very—what's the word I'm looking for—not "entrepreneurial," it's not quite right. We would not be an entrepreneurial family, but a bootstrap family, I guess. My grandmother would be an inspiration. . . . There are a lot of parallels between her life and the lives of the women that we support. She grew up on a farm. She went through sixth or seventh grade only because that's what the family could afford to send her to. No running water in her house, no heating, none of those things. And she had to go out and eventually she did start her own business in catering that she used to support herself. . . . So I would say our view of the world is shaped by that experience not only because it was women driven, but also because it was about taking advantage of opportunities.

Mirroring the story of the Deatons, leaders of other grassroots INGOs spoke of the need for aid recipients to seize opportunities.[18] A board member of Wellsprings of Hope expressed her frustration that a Ugandan boy to whom she had provided a scholarship had failed his exit examination for three consecutive years. When she visited Uganda, the boy explained that he would be more successful if he could attend a boarding school rather than walking from home each morning. "I really had some serious discussions with him when I was there last year. 'I understand it's hard, but you have to take advantage of this. . . . You have to raise your grades before I'm gonna spend that extra money to send you to boarding school.'" Erasto and other immigrants volunteering with grassroots INGOs often emphasize education—a critical element of their own mobility—even though the possibilities for using their own educations were radically expanded by immigration. But education is still portrayed as a path to success for those who remain in developing countries. Vicki, who had emigrated from Ukraine as a child and now volunteers for a women's entrepreneurship organization writes on their website, "While my family was able to move to the US in hopes of a brighter future, such opportunities are almost unheard of in Southern India and many other parts of the world. It is this personal experience, along with my passion for helping others and my career skill set that will allow me to not only help women understand their personal and business finances, but will allow me to offer emotional support" (Women's Entrepreneurship Initiative).

What Vicki describes must be understood as more nuanced than an impulse to "pay it forward." Of the host of ways she might offer support to those who remain in need of a "brighter future," she settles on a particular set of skills that will be as useful to women in India as they are to middle-class Americans: knowledge of personal and business finances in order to run a small business. The founder of Indego Africa also emphasized individual business skills as the most important thing he could offer. Later in recounting the story of his grandmother, Matt specifically mentioned the public amenities that allowed his grandmother to raise three sons successfully. But politics and public goods did not enter the blueprint for Indego Africa: When I asked what made him move away from a model more focused on institution building rather than developing human capital, he spoke of passing on the business acumen of his family: "I think that the actual conduct of economic activity in business is really healthy and we—and I think that was also where our experience came from, because really this was in many ways a joint project between my father and I in the beginning—*so I would say we were quite keen to pass on some of the skills and knowledge that we had* [emphasis added]. We thought like actually helping them conduct business was a valuable form of training." In other words, while Matt drew inspiration from the story of his grandmother—one he knew had political and other contextual particulars—when it was time to decide what an aid organization in Rwanda would actually do, he turned to the skills that he had that he felt were most useful.

"[T]o be an open door for people to come and serve" was how the founder of For Kenya's Tomorrow succinctly described what grassroots INGOs offer American supporters that mainstream NGOs do not. Grassroots INGOs allow amateurs to take an active role in aid work, to build projects around their skills and their ideas of how development proceeds. This logic of building around the skills and interests of the volunteers fits the profile of a supply-driven organization. And while these groups are interested in seeing instrumental goals achieved—more children educated, fewer families living in poverty—the process of *how* those goals are achieved is essential to why Americans support the organization. These are *expressive* organizations. As St. David's Relief demonstrated, volunteers see themselves "changed," or note that their work was meaningful because "there was no massive bureaucracy doling out huge amounts of materials." Instead, "the humanitarian aid was given face to face."

With grassroots INGOs offering American supporters these opportunities, what does the aid look like? The next chapter elaborates three models of grassroots aid and compares them with the approaches of mainstream aid organizations.

4 *Provide and Transform*

Grassroots INGOs' Models of Aid

If grassroots INGO aid is shaped by volunteers' experiences and interests, what does the aid actually look like, and how is it different from what NGOs have done before? And what are the implications of this kind of aid for development?

To make sense of how grassroots INGOs approach aid, we need to go beyond descriptive statistics of the projects these groups undertake and whom they serve. One of David Korten's most useful insights about NGO work is that every organization, whether it realizes it or not, has a theory of change. NGO interventions are built around basic, sometimes tacit, beliefs about what is needed for development to happen. For mainstream NGOs, these theories can be shaped by practical lessons learned from on-the-ground experience, or they can be more instrumental responses to the development paradigms in vogue with the agencies that fund them. The employees of mainstream NGOs also are members of a professional field where knowledge passes formally through training and informally as colleagues learn from each other on shared projects or in evening conversations in expatriate bars.[1] When these theories of development must be translated into projects, NGOs' approaches to development are ultimately influenced by their resource constraints—in particular their financial and technical capacity. They rely on donors to fund their work and local brokers and beneficiaries to help them carry it out.

Grassroots international NGOs are shaped by different resources and ideas. While their leaders might absorb development paradigms of the World Bank or USAID from what they read in blogs or newspapers, there is no pressure to perform these priorities in grant applications. Instead, volunteers' own skills, ideas, and emotional experiences are the resources around which programs are built. The previous chapter showed that the distinctive feature of grassroots INGOs is the opportunity they offer amateurs to build personal relationships and contribute their own labor and skills to aid. Volunteer labor is abundant, but it is often confined to stints of weeks during particular times of the year. While these groups avoid the contingencies of the grant economy, they work within the limits of individual donations and must show donors that even their small contributions are making a difference. Grassroots INGOs have neither the technical capacity nor the obligation to carry out formal monitoring and evaluation schemes for donors. But they do need to show something for their work, and in practice that often translates to photos of things built or narratives of individual lives changed. In this chapter I connect the resources and constraints of grassroots INGOs elaborated in previous chapters to the approaches to aid that the organizations offer.

Inspired by Korten's "generations" typology, I describe here three models of grassroots INGO aid. Like Korten's models, mine are distinguished by the unifying idea of what is needed to make development happen. I developed these models inductively from the website sample, beginning with the sectors of the projects that grassroots INGOs describe on their sites. Chapter 2 showed that these projects ranged from building schools to distributing food to supporting theater troupes. I found that these projects could be distilled into three broad types, depending on the grassroots INGO's point of intervention. The first model I describe below worked on "stuff"; the second worked on individuals; the third worked on broader social relationships. Once each grassroots INGO was classified according to its point of intervention, I saw that characteristic patterns emerged for recipients, rationales, and roles for American supporters. As in chapter 2, *rationales* are defined as discursive acts that explain why something was done. In the context of aid groups' websites, they are most often making an explicit claim of why particular people should be helped or why a particular intervention is appropriate. *Recipient* descriptions include both status designations (men, women, children/youth, orphans), and qualitative descriptions of aid recipients. Finally, *roles for US supporters* refer to descriptions of action already taken by supporters or appeals for readers of the website to offer particular kinds of support to the organization. In this analysis all 150 organizations are assigned to one model according to its primary sector of work as determined by the qualitative coding. The frequencies of each of these variables in each of the three models are given in table 12.

Distilling the work of grassroots INGOs into these three models helps us understand in a more substantive way how these groups approach aid. The similarities and differences from Korten's models emerge and are striking because these organizations were all found roughly in the same era; they don't, for the most part, represent different cohorts of NGOs. I describe each model in turn before considering the main implication of these models: that the majority of grassroots INGOs approach development as a personal process.

TABLE 12. Frequencies of Codes for Rationales, Recipients, and Roles for US Supporters by Aid Model

	Goods and Services	Skills and Dispositions	Social Relations
Rationales			
Suffering*	38%	38%	6%
God's purposes*	35%	13%	16%
Following international authority	17%	18%	25%
Epidemic	15%	4%	6%
War	13%	13%	9%
Natural disaster	11%	2%	0%
Human rights*	11%	16%	32%
Political strife	9%	18%	19%
Justice	8%	16%	19%
Outside oppression*	3%	2%	44%
Gender inequality*	2%	22%	6%
Recipients: Status Categories			
Children/youth*	57%	73%	37%
Orphans*	44%	18%	6%
Women	29%	49%	38%
Men	8%	11%	25%
Recipients: Personal Qualities			
Deprived*	47%	47%	13%
Vulnerable	19%	20%	13%
Kind/good/hospitable	15%	20%	19%
Has future ambitions*	13%	29%	12%
Shared humanity*	13%	24%	0%
Hardworking*	12%	49%	13%
Referred to by work role	2%	11%	6%
Roles for US Supporters			
Donate money*	90%	100%	75%
Donate goods	28%	27%	6%
Pray	17%	7%	6%
Volunteer in US	28%	44%	31%
Volunteer abroad	35%	40%	25%
Total n	89	45	16

*Differences between models significant at p< .05 (Pearson's chi-squared test)

Model #1: Direct Provision of Goods and Services

The most common model of aid (used by 60 percent of grassroots INGOs in the sample) is direct provision of the goods and services that poor people lack. This can involve distributing the necessities of life, like food and clothing, either in the aftermath of a disaster or to the chronically needy. It also includes building housing or providing the sorts of infrastructure and services that are often provided by the public sector in developed countries: medical clinics and care, water, electricity, and orphanages or foster homes. In other words, organizations working in this model stand in for the family or the state.

The sophistication with which these goods and services are distributed varies. Some organizations collect small items like pencils or soccer balls to be distributed as gifts to beneficiaries. Other organizations provide more sophisticated and large-scale redistributive schemes for American surplus items, like the several library projects that move English-language books by the shipping container to Africa. The provision of services can be more durable, such as when grassroots INGOs build wells or clinics. Teams of visiting medical personnel typically donate their time and bring extra supplies with them, sometimes offering training in new techniques to their local counterparts.

Disaster relief organizations are part of this aid model. For mainstream NGOs with capabilities like cargo flights or pop-up hospitals, the distinction between relief (short-term assistance) and development (long-term transformation) operations is apparent. The difference is less clear for grassroots aid groups. In a typical example, an organization that had made previous contact with a pastor in Haiti sent volunteers with donated stocks of clothing and medical supplies after the 2010 earthquake. As the months went on, volunteers would continue to come and would assist in an orphanage established by the pastor. For these grassroots INGOs both relief and development objectives were accomplished either by providing goods and services directly from American volunteers or by privately funding local efforts with American donations.

Though the boundary between relief and development tasks can be ambiguous for grassroots INGOs, the way they portray their beneficiaries is distinct. Websites featuring relief projects rarely differentiate among aid recipients. But when grassroots INGOs are working on development, they tend to emphasize marginalized populations—women, children, the sick—in their discourse. For all recipients, the rationales for aid tend to emphasize suffering. Compared with other models of aid, organizations working in this model rarely appeal to abstract principles (e.g., human rights) or elaborate political causes of disadvantage. Aid groups working in the goods and services model most often rely on the rationale of addressing suffering, as in the following text: "In Senegal, and in much of Africa, there is a season that we do not experience . . . The Hungry Season. In many rural villages, families are reduced to one meal a day, and not even that. The hardship goes largely unnoticed because it is not a widespread famine. . . . It is just a slow, gnawing, debilitating hunger that robs people of their energy and strength." Then, the organization makes the claim for how their work is positioned to alleviate the suffering: "We at Andando hope we can be a small part of the solution. We are working at creating an environment in rural villages where people have enhanced ability to grow their own food, through micro lending, water security and education. There are no quick solutions, but village by village we hope to make a small difference along the way" (Andando).

The response that suffering seems to demand, according to this discourse, offers roles for Americans. These roles include the donation of goods and the logistical management of their transport from the United States. American volunteers may also offer low-skill work (painting a new school building) or high-skill interventions (volunteer doctors). These groups justify their presence by the imperative of the human need and the absence of local providers: "Cameroon's East region is sometimes characterized as 'forgotten' by politicians and development projects. . . . Its 'forgotten' status is one major reason why Opportunity Africa chose to concentrate our work in the East" (Opportunity Africa). Yet sometimes the roles for volunteers that these pressing needs seem to suggest are at odds with the prescriptions of development experts, such as when volunteers are invited to play for days or weeks with children at orphanages—a practice UNICEF now condemns as damaging to children's well-being.[2]

The goods and services model aligns in many respects with Korten's "first generation" model of aid. Grassroots INGOs working in this model address acute needs with direct provision, and raise support by conveying the suffering of their clients and the need for immediate aid. Because all needs are portrayed as acute, the donation of goods and volunteer labor—even low-skilled labor—is framed as useful. Whether or not grassroots INGO leaders consider it privately, their public materials neglect the long-term effects in receiving countries of importing goods like clothing, medical supplies, or sports equipment that might be purchased locally; nor is discussion often given to how beneficiaries fare when volunteer service providers return home.[3] In sum, grassroots INGOs in this group provide new, decentralized channels to transfer human and material resources from the United States to needy individuals in the Global South.

Model #2: Skills and Dispositions

If the goods and services model can crudely be characterized as the "give a man a fish," approach to development, the second model is about teaching a man to fish—specifically, to have both the skills and the *initiative* to fish. What unifies this model is the attempt to alter aid recipients' thinking and behavior—their desires, their habits, their strategies—so that they can eventually prosper on their own. Within this model I include two sorts of projects: education and small business. There are differences in the targeted recipients and the techniques of intervention, but the unifying thread is an effort toward transforming the dispositions and behavior of recipients. Therefore, by definition, the model is aimed squarely at individuals rather than collectivities.

Thirty percent of all grassroots INGOs in the sample primarily work in this model. They give training for small business or offer microcredit, or provide education by directly operating schools, offering scholarships, or running summer enrichment programs. The targeted recipients vary. Education projects target youth, predictably, while small business programs often target women. What all programs have in common is the discourse of transformation. Small business and microcredit organizations strive to build people's sense of initiative, risk-taking, and future planning. The aim is that entrepreneurial individuals will seize market opportunities and reap material and social gains. Small business and microcredit programs are depicted as offering women social empowerment vis-à-vis men; as providing self-esteem and dignity; as generating leadership qualities; and as driving overall change—economic and social—in communities.

Education programs also aim to cultivate a work ethic and agile mind, though the particular tasks to which an educated youth will apply these traits is left unspecified. The theme is that an educated person is one that can "break the cycle of poverty." The language of transformation is prevalent here as it is with business projects: "Education offers children a way out of the cycle of poverty by giving children a broader range of choices for their lives. It provides individuals with the necessary tools to transcend poverty, to participate in their communities, and to provide a higher quality of life for themselves and future generations" (Wings of Peace).

In both the education and small business variants of this model, Americans tend to play complementary roles that offer incentives to the new subjectivities of aid recipients: they offer scholarships, or act as buyers for the products (e.g., fair-trade coffee or artisan goods) that the nascent businesspeople market. Organizations working in this model were more likely than those in the goods and services model to cite as rationales abstract principles of human rights, justice, or gender equality. These are rationales that emphasize the *sameness* between recipients and donors rather than their differences, even as the projects themselves aim to make recipients more like donors. Even when organizations use religious rationales, their discourse too emphasizes sameness: "We do not want to go with the attitude of 'doing' but of being with our friends, to learn from each other, to pray with and encourage each other, to partner with what God is already doing there. While we hope to accomplish a lot, we also hope to spend our time building relationships with Malawians, each other, and with God" (Circle of Hope International).

This idea that aid-givers and receivers are fundamentally the same—in their rights, in their potential, in their dreams—supports the proposition that the skills and dispositions that have made aid-givers successful in the United States will be useful in developing countries. Grassroots INGOs providing goods and services work under the theory that transferring stuff from North to South is the key to development. Groups working in the second model assume that transferring ways of thinking and being is the key, and that the stuff will follow once the people are transformed.

Since personal transformation is the goal of these projects, recipients' personal stories are indicators of success. Grassroots INGOs using this model of aid are more apt than in any other to highlight recipients' personal stories on their websites. For example:

Clarisse graduated near the top of her class in high school and wanted nothing more than to become a nurse. Unfortunately, her widowed mother did not have the means to pay for nursing school. Opportunity Africa provided a full scholarship to Clarisse for nursing school, and assisted her in the job search process after graduating. She successfully landed a position at the Ministry of Health as an HIV/AIDS educator in the rural areas of Eastern Cameroon (Opportunity Africa).

Candida's farm and all of the producers' farms in the Cosurca Cooperative are located in the most dangerous region of Colombia. In this region, the FARC guerillas roam through the communities, bringing violence, bloodshed, and murder. The sad fact is that 30 percent of the producers are now women alone, their husbands having been murdered due to the violence and drug trafficking in the region. Candida did not want to grow coca on her farm; she is smiling now because with Café Femenino, she no longer needs to grow coca. Her coffee plants may not produce as much income for her, but Café Femenino gives her and all the women producers a life of dignity without fear of being arrested by the police. Café Femenino is also providing hope of a better future to these women (Café Femenino).

These narratives trace the transformation of recipients' material circumstances but also their hopes and plans for the future. Groups working in this model give far more attention to recipients' personal qualities on their websites than the other models. These organizations are particularly apt to emphasize recipients' future ambitions and work ethic.

This model shares several common traits with Korten's "second generation" approach. It turns from outside provision to stimulating local people to become self-reliant by cultivating new skills and attitudes. As in Korten's model, grassroots INGOs working in this model assume that "inertia can be broken through the intervention of an outside change agent who helps the community realize its potentials."[4] But Korten's second generation involves a shift from the individual as unit of intervention to the community or some collectivity, while grassroots INGOs working on skills and dispositions remain steadfastly focused on individuals. Korten notes variety among second-generation strategies in the degree to which they focus on human resource development or on empowerment as related to local power relationships. Many grassroots INGOs in this model do little to focus on collective subjectivities or how individual skills operate in broader contexts of power and resources.

Model #3: Social Relations

This model, which characterizes the work of roughly one out of ten grassroots INGOs, involves strengthening social groups or building relations between groups. The development issues that these groups emphasize are policy advocacy, capacity building, democratization, cultural exchange, and preserving cultural heritage. When grassroots INGOs work on such projects, they are often providing cash support for a cultural collective like an indigenous people's group or a Tibetan monastery. Cultural exchange groups such as Partners of the Americas also fall into this category. Other groups mainly aim to raise Americans' awareness of human rights or cultural issues of their developing-country partners. While improving the standard of living might be a long-term goal, the more immediate intervention is to allow people in the Global South to build collective skills or relationships that will empower them.

Organizations that aim to alter recipients' relationships with institutions or other social groups face a fundamentally different task than those that aim to provide social services or needed goods. Here the needs and aspirations of individuals recede in favor of the fates of some collectivity. Unlike most other grassroots INGOs, many of these groups engage in advocacy before the public and elected officials in the United States and developing countries. Human Dignity International (formerly Christian Solidarity International) is part of an international coalition of groups advocating for the rights of Christian minorities outside of the West. The Washington Kurdish Institute advocates for the Kurdish ethnic minority in Iraq, while two organizations in the sample combine general political advocacy for Tibetan people with support for Tibetan Buddhist institutions in exile. The theme here is that these organizations are supporting the rights of political minorities. Of all of the organizations in the sample, these are the most explicitly political; they are led by well-educated members of diasporas and have strong political constituencies in the United States. But rather than engaging directly in politics in developing countries, these organizations operate in the manner of Keck and Sikkink's transnational advocacy groups, leveraging connections among influential allies (in this case in the United States, though some of these groups also have branches in Europe) for their political ends. They operate at the margins permitted within designation as a 501(c)3 public charity, so their public language must be carefully chosen to remain within the discursive framework of human rights advocacy rather than political lobbying.[5]

Other organizations aim to build more equitable and collaborative relationships between Americans and communities in the Global South through exchange and service programs. The Wallace Toronto Foundation, Global Routes, and Minnesota Uruguay Partners (a Partners of the Americas chapter) all operate exchange or volunteer trips for Americans to communities in the Global South.[6] While the American visitors often take part in some service project, that project is a means to the broader end of international friendship and solidarity. In the case of the Wallace Toronto Foundation, the social groups whose relationships are to be transformed can be pinpointed: the goal is to improve relations between the Church of Jesus Christ of Latter-day Saints (LDS) and the Czech and Slovak republics. Mormon missionaries had fled the country in World War II and returned, according to official accounts, after the fall of the iron curtain. The Toronto foundation, named for the founding LDS missionary in Czechoslovakia, returns with volunteer groups each summer to engage in a service project designated by municipal leaders. Foundation volunteers also assisted in the petition effort for legal recognition of the LDS church under Slovak law.

The discourse of groups working in social relations is markedly different from grassroots INGOs working through other models.

Since their level of intervention is more often collectivities than individuals, there is less discourse about the moral character of individual recipients. The rationales for this sort of work are distinctly different than other models. The appeal to alleviate suffering, the most common rationale among the other aid types, is almost entirely absent here. The websites of these groups were more likely to emphasize political strife (19%) or outside oppression (44%) as the rationale for aid. Advocacy groups, in particular, are willing to blame national governments, parties, or even individual politicians for social ills. This is in stark contrast to the majority of grassroots INGOs, whose explanations for why recipients need help almost never assign blame to any particular actor.

Compared with grassroots INGOs working in other models, there is less role for American cash or in-kind donations for these groups. Like other sorts of grassroots INGOs, groups working in this model rely on volunteers for administration. But they also seek Americans to act as hosts for foreign visitors or to engage in advocacy, and they are less likely than other types of grassroots INGOs to solicit Americans to volunteer abroad. These organizations are older on average than those working in other models: the median founding year for these organizations is 1999, compared to a median founding year of 2008 for both the goods and services and skills and dispositions models. Taken together, these traits show that grassroots INGOs that operate on social relations are a more heterogeneous group, and diverge from other groups in the way that they engage Americans in "getting their hands dirty" and in interacting with recipients.

Social relations organizations bear some resemblance to both Korten's second- and third- generation strategies. They are second-generation-like in their emphasis on empowerment and in recognizing that local contexts should determine development priorities. Like third-generation organizations, these groups attempt to influence national policies. Grassroots INGOs operating in this mode are mainly allies, bringing financial resources and public voice to social groups in a developing country. But their effectiveness is constrained by their budgets and the relatively shallow legitimacy of their relationship with their partners. Of the three models of aid that grassroots INGOs use, the social relations model is the rarest and the least like the others. Americans have less of a hands-on role, there is less contact with individuals in the aid-receiving country, and there is a greater role for politics and policy.

Development as a Personal Process

The vast majority of grassroots INGOs—89 percent—work from the goods and services or the skills and dispositions models of aid. The rest work from the social relations model, which aims to achieve long-term development by strengthening collectivities or building social relations between groups. By making their unit of intervention a group rather than the individual, and by working on projects that put these groups in political contexts and contestations, organizations working in the social relations model approach development differently than most grassroots INGOs. The dominant goods and services and skills and dispositions models of aid differ in their projects, discourse, and roles for US supporters, but they are ultimately similar in their vision of how development takes place. Thus, while acknowledging the divergence of a minority of organizations, I argue that grassroots INGOs have a discernable vision of *development as a personal process*.

To approach development as a personal process means, first, that grassroots INGOs see the heroic individual as the agent of change. Americans whose skills and voluntarism would be rejected by professionalized NGOs are made the lifeblood of grassroots INGOs. Rather than depicting American volunteers as being short on time, language skills, and knowledge of the local context, grassroots INGOs celebrate volunteers as intrepid travelers, compassionate souls, and holders of needed labor and crucial knowledge. Many websites emphasize that anyone can be useful as a volunteer: those with high skills can be facilitated by a local interpreter; those willing to do manual labor or play with children demonstrate solidarity; even those who donate cast-off goods or pray for the project are making a difference. Emphasizing the generosity of volunteers allows organizations to ignore the fact that some of their work is frivolous (e.g., distributing toys or giving haircuts), could be more efficiently done by local labor (e.g., building houses), or is even damaging to recipients (e.g., short-term helping in orphanages).

Aid recipients are also portrayed as heroes, especially when organizations work in the skills and dispositions model. These heroic recipients are typically the highly motivated student or the hardworking woman who builds a business to provide for her family. Websites are flush with the personal narratives of individuals who transform their lives with the help of aid projects. One quarter of the websites in the goods and services model and a third in the skills and dispositions model recounted the personal stories of aid recipients. These aid recipients are most often characterized as hardworking and ambitious; the narratives often describe how a scholarship or loan or training program was the catalyst that released the person's potential. Stories abound of scholarship recipients who go on to train as nurses or teachers, thus accelerating their countries' development.

Grassroots INGOs' tacit theory of change is that investing in the right individuals will yield broader improvements. Yspaniola, for example, writes, "For every dollar that a woman earns in the developing world, she invests eighty cents into her family. Our work empowers women, thereby creating healthier families and communities. . . . By supporting universal literacy and higher education, our programs empower our recipients with the skills to provide for their families and the capacity to become leaders and advocates for social justice in their communities and family."

Ethnographic research has shown how context frustrates the relationship between individual empowerment and development outcomes. Yspaniola's mission statement for women in the Dominican Republic echoes the rhetoric of "empowerment" that Swidler and Watkins observed in HIV programs in Malawi. Drawing on the logic of the feminist movements in the United States and Europe, these programs assumed that Malawian women with legal and economic parity with men would be able to bargain with their partners as equals, and so be less vulnerable to risky sex. Empowerment was assumed to be the key to better health outcomes. But in fact, HIV rates were higher among the wealthy and the urban, among both men and women. Therefore, Swidler and Watkins argue, programs that really wanted to reduce HIV transmission to vulnerable women would have encouraged them to marry young in rural areas and to remain there.[7] Jill DeTemple observed the unintended outcomes of an economic empowerment project in Ecuador that trained women as cheese makers. For a time, the project thrived, but social norms and the lack of labor-saving technology dictated that the women continue their childcare and domestic responsibilities. They eventually abandoned the cheese-making project in exhaustion.[8] These findings point to problems grassroots INGOs are likely to encounter when they do not consider how the new skills or dispositions they promote actually align with local contexts.

Stories of aid recipients who go on to change their communities are an essential part of grassroots INGOs' vision of development. Broader social change is imagined to happen through contagion as well-trained individuals go on spreading their knowledge, gradually developing the nation from the bottom up. This theory emerged in case-study interviews to describe the impact of ultrasound-trained doctors, children educated in personal hygiene, religious primary schools, religious evangelism, village health workers, and youth in politics. On their websites, grassroots INGOs rarely describe ambitions to change the world; but they frequently write of trying to "change lives." The texts describe these changed lives as going on, in turn, to affect others. One website asked donors to imagine the potential impact that a child educated with a scholarship might have: "one of these students could grow up to be the next Martin Luther King or Oprah Winfrey!" (San Alfonso Mission) Even groups like Yspaniola, with humbler ambitions, assume that individual skills will somehow translate into "the capacity to become leaders and advocates for social justice in their families and communities." How? Yspaniola, like most grassroots INGOs, neglects how individual capacity becomes collective capacity.

While turning to local civic or political institutions would be an obvious possibility, many grassroots INGOs minimize the role of collectivities and deliberately avoid government. In grassroots INGOs' theory of development, the institutional role of the state is minimized. Instead, government is seen as a perch on which powerful persons sit, and the quality of government hinges on the character of these individuals. In interviews, volunteers' discussions of government centered on corruption, which was framed as fundamentally a problem of character. When asked about the roles that government should play in development, respondents often spoke of government officials in terms of their personal integrity or as role models for citizens. One volunteer cited the presence of a government official at a ceremony for a private school opened by an NGO as providing an inspirational message for the children there: "I thought that was a very positive thing, to see somebody who was a Ugandan in a position, first off, a woman, who is educated, and is in a position of power, talking to them about their rights" (Jackie, Wellsprings of Hope). In an extreme example of focus on personal character, one volunteer explained the predatory reign of Idi Amin as damaging because of the example it set of sexual immorality: "I think that the reign of Idi Amin damaged that country so badly. He was a very poor role model as a father and as a husband; had many wives, and didn't—you know he encouraged men to just take as many wives as they wanted and—he was very corrupt" (Frances, Wellsprings of Hope).

Grassroots INGO volunteers alternatively depict the state as feeble or as a site of corruption and an impediment to the direct transactions between aid givers and receivers. The volunteers described their work as taking the place of government services: "it's really stepping into the gap of what the government can't or won't do" (Frances, Wellsprings of Hope). Yet when local or national governments attempted to fold grassroots INGO efforts into broader development schemes or to exert political control over their projects, the volunteers I interviewed expressed frustration at what they saw as unnecessary roadblocks to the primary goal of providing services and transferring knowledge. That transfer, to the recipients identified by the grassroots INGO, often took precedence over the development of local institutions that could provide those services over the long term.

. . .

How do grassroots INGOs approach development? This chapter showed that a minority of organizations focuses on the social relations that affect development by engaging in advocacy, supporting cultural heritage, or building cultural exchanges between groups. The most common type of organization aims to directly provide goods and services to the underserved, taking on the responsibilities of the family or the state. By using discourse that emphasizes the suffering of aid recipients, they encourage impatience with politics and local solutions. Another common approach is to transmit the skills and dispositions—educated and market-oriented—that Americans understand to be essential to socioeconomic mobility. These organizations highlight the personal qualities of dedication and optimism in their recipients. In justifying their work, they appeal to abstract principles of gender equality and human rights, using arguments that emphasize the similarities of aid donors and recipients.

The dominant models of aid used by grassroots INGOs are second- or even first-generation approaches in David Korten's typology—that is, approaches that were abandoned by mainstream NGOs by the 1970s. Except for humanitarian emergencies, larger NGOs have largely given up providing goods and services. This is not to say such projects aren't wanted by recipients. Ethnographic accounts have shown how recipients strategically navigate second- and third-generation programs to acquire tangible goods like boreholes, chicken feed, and bicycles.[9] The goods and services that grassroots INGOs provide are often needed and very welcome by the people who receive them.

Although some grassroots INGO programs are "giving fish" and others are "teaching fishing," there are deeper similarities. Most of these groups approach development as a personal process. Heroic individuals are the agents of change who go on to effect broader social transformation through contagion. Government is usually to be carefully navigated around rather than engaged with. While the personal transformations of aid recipients are celebrated, there is a risk here. Programs that center on personal change—especially change that is meant to make aid recipients have the skills and dispositions of American volunteers—do not always take into account the local contexts in which that "changed" person operates. Nor do projects to provide goods and services always consider how locally funded and managed institutions might more sustainably provide those services.

Grassroots INGOs can learn to take account of these issues, as the Rwanda Ultrasound Initiative did. Rather than directly providing medical care, RUI agreed to become a continuing medical education provider for the Rwandan Ministry of Health. Under this agreement, the Ministry of Health has the right to approve their curriculum and harmonize it with other medical training in the country, and to allocate trainees according to the health care system's needs. At the Ministry of Health's prodding, RUI thus has to adapt what it teaches to fit the local context and not merely to be whatever skills the US doctors would like to teach. And rather than doctors flocking to whatever paid training session is on offer from an NGO, Rwandan doctors can be assigned to RUI's programs or to another continuing education program—in either case taking into account the staffing needs of public hospitals.

But more commonly, grassroots INGOs avoid government or other local collectivities as a means to sustained change. Without engaging these institutions, and without committing themselves to perpetual support, grassroots INGOs have little choice but to hope that changed people will change the world.

5 *Resources, Relationships, and Accountability*

Wellsprings of Hope faced a crisis two years after its founding. For several months, Bill, the American pastor who started the organization, had been getting messages from the Ugandan pastors who led the projects saying that something was amiss with the group's finances. They suspected that one of their fellow pastors was siphoning money. That pastor had recently taken a second wife and had made some extravagant purchases; meanwhile, Wellsprings' books weren't adding up. The Americans on the board expressed their concern to Bill. *If this can't be straightened out*, they told him, *our congregation can't continue to support this organization.* Bill flew to Uganda for a—literal—come-to-Jesus meeting with the suspected embezzler. He presented the evidence of malfeasance and asked the pastor to make a public confession and resignation before the Ugandan congregations and his fellow pastors. The confession was tearfully made. Spiritual reconciliation was granted, but the pastor, whom Bill had described as one of his "best friends," was exiled from the organization and forced to hand over Wellsprings of Hope's stamp, the group's marker of official status in all Ugandan documents. In the following months Bill and the American board of directors created new guidelines for the management of

Wellsprings' books and communications: financial reports had to be submitted in a standard spreadsheet on agreed-upon dates, and all email communication between the Ugandan pastors and the American board had to cc at least one other pastor. With these guidelines in place, the American congregation agreed to continue its financial support.

This story of near disaster illustrates three themes about personal relationships among grassroots INGO leaders, donors in the United States, and partners in the aid-receiving community. First, the relationships between leaders and their American friends and family are critical for gathering resources, since grassroots INGOs rely almost entirely on gifts from groups and individuals that the leaders know personally. The majority of Wellsprings' budget came from the Texas congregation and those members' friends. If they had financially abandoned the NGO, it would have folded. Second, leaders' relationships with friends or relatives in the aid-receiving countries becomes crucial for implementing the projects. These friends abroad often become *brokers* for the organizations—middlemen who are trusted to get things done on the ground. In this case, the pastors, whom Bill described as some of his best friends, were responsible for implementing and monitoring Wellsprings' projects and for communicating any local problems to the American board. With Americans visiting only weeks every year, it took years of chronic financial impropriety by one of these Ugandan brokers before anything was visible to the donors.

Third, these sets of relationships structure grassroots INGOs' accountabilities. A local employee skimming church ladies' donations to support a lavish lifestyle is the stereotypical problem pointing to the need for NGO accountability. But who is an NGO accountable to, exactly? This story suggests several possible answers. The Ugandan leaders were accountable to one another, but also to the US board of directors (most especially their founder). The board of directors felt keenly accountable to its donors. The Ugandan and American leaders felt accountable to the community where the group worked (thus the demand for the public apology). The concern over the group's official stamp suggests accountability to the Ugandan government and public at large. Donors, directors, clients, the public—all are potential stakeholders in NGO work.

Determining whom NGOs are accountable to is a sticky question compared with the relatively clear lines of accountability in public and for-profit organizations. Democratically elected governments are accountable to citizens through their votes. Private firms are accountable to their shareholders, who have clear indications of the firm's success in profits and losses. In the nonprofit sector—among which we count NGOs, including grassroots INGOs—probably the strongest legal case can be made that the "principal" to whom the organization is accountable is the board of directors. But unlike private firms, nonprofits' revenues come from sources other than the customers: charitable donors. One could argue that a prudent nonprofit that wanted to maintain its financial support should therefore be accountable to the wishes of the donors. But nonprofits derive their legal and moral legitimacy from producing some charitable good for beneficiaries. Whether those beneficiaries receive donated blood, education, or medical care, shouldn't they be able to hold the nonprofit accountable for the quality of those goods? The problem takes on added complexity for NGOs that operate across national borders. The governments of countries in which NGOs work can make a fair claim that they are responsible for the public well-being in their country, and that NGOs must be accountable to them. It becomes quickly apparent that NGOs have many stakeholders, each of whom—say, the government of Kenya, the inhabitants of a Nairobi slum, and the rural Americans that donate to a grassroots INGO— could make opposing claims on the organization.

Edwards and Hulme have classified NGOs' accountability into *upward* and *downward* varieties.[1] Upward accountability is to donors and governments, and is the kind most often practiced by NGOs. Even very small NGOs provide their donors with financial records and basic reports of their activities.[2] NGOs registered as tax-exempt organizations in the United States face basic legal accountability to the Internal Revenue Service. Groups with more than $50,000 per year must file a Form 990 that describes their income and expenditures, including salaries paid and foreign entities funded. Even groups with incomes less than $50,000 must file a shorter, electronic disclosure or risk losing their tax-exempt status. Most developing countries have developed forms of legal accountability for NGOs by requiring that the organizations register with a national office, a form of accountability that appears to be strengthening in many countries as part of the "closing space" for civil society.[3] In practice, however, the official registration of NGOs is a very loose form of accountability for small NGOs. Field research has shown that only a fraction of registered NGOs in developing countries can be actually located (suggesting that many have disbanded) and that, of NGOs physically encountered in the field, only a fraction were registered (suggesting that many never register in the first place).[4]

Downward accountability relates to the obligations of an NGO to its beneficiaries. NGOs can be accountable to beneficiaries in several ways: by being transparent about where money is coming from and how it is being spent; by demonstrating meaningful results for its projects; or by inviting public participation in setting priorities and designing projects. The participation of beneficiaries in the choosing and running of aid projects has become nearly sacrosanct in development work.[5] But a great deal of research has shown the difficulties of meaningfully involving beneficiary communities in the planning and execution of development projects. White, Ebrahim, and others describe skim-milk approaches to participation that amount to little more than public notification of projects that have been designed at headquarters; aid organizations might insist on the convening of village meetings or committees for "consultation" to approve plans that have been chosen by a handful of elites.[6] A major evaluation by the World Bank of participatory approaches found that most efforts at participation failed to improve the results of the projects.[7] Participation, like all things holy, can become a hollow ritual.

The first part of this chapter draws on the five case study organizations to examine the relationship between the grassroots INGOs' leaders and their American supporters. It shows that relying on friends and family to maintain an NGO has advantages, among them a flexible form of upward accountability. Unlike NGOs or domestic nonprofits that bear huge administrative burdens from their funders, grassroots INGOs operate on a relational upward accountability in which the personal trust that donors have for the leaders substitutes for formal reporting requirements. Wellsprings' donors requested only the barest formal measures of accountability until thousands of dollars disappeared into an employee's pocket. Loose measures of accountability also free grassroots INGOs from donor-driven development—the need to select projects based on the approaches en vogue with aid donors.[8] Grassroots INGOs have the freedom to pursue the projects that appeal to its leaders, and not simply to pursue projects for which they can measure their success and "prove" their effectiveness.

The second part of the chapter turns to the relationships between grassroots INGOs and beneficiary communities. These personal relationships often motivate Americans to become involved in aid, and the partners in developing countries take on the role of broker. Narratives from Wellsprings of Hope, Activate Tanzania, and For Kenya's Tomorrow show that these relationships serve practical and emotional goals, but strains emerge. In grassroots INGOs the strong personal ties between Americans and brokers obscures the fact that the parties are involved in a peculiar principal-agent relationship. Brokers are friends or family members of the American leaders, and are presumed to be acting on the leaders' behalf, in the best interest of the grassroots INGO. Yet these brokers are also expected to provide the "local" perspective—to speak on behalf of the beneficiary community. Downward accountability is shaped by the dual agency position of grassroots INGOs' brokers; these individuals struggle to simultaneously convey the interests of the beneficiaries and the American volunteers. I conclude by arguing that grassroots INGOs could engage in a form of downward accountability that is less about monitoring and more about developing shared goals. But grassroots INGOs must move away from reliance on brokers for local feedback, and I show how this might be done by pointing to the approaches of two of the case study organizations.

Relationships with American Family and Friends

Grassroots INGOs are built on the gifts of the founders' friends and family. Matt Mitro began Indego Africa by sending out an email to forty family members and friends. Natalie wrote to the church members and relatives who had supported her short-term mission trips, and Activate Tanzania relied on Erasto's colleagues and a gift from Kate's uncle. The typical grassroots INGO operates on less than $25,000 per year.[9] Both the website and case study evidence show that the money typically comes from individual donations, most often from the family, friends, or colleagues of the NGOs' American leaders.

Even though practically every website in the sample made an appeal for cash donations, these sites showed that personal networks were the organizations' financial backbone. Over one-quarter of grassroots INGO websites showed family members—often husbands and wives, but sometimes siblings or parents and children—working together as volunteers.[10] Websites illustrated the personal ties between leaders and the groups' most common US partners—religious congregations, business donors, and artists or artist organizations. Grassroots INGO volunteers often turned to their own religious communities for recurring financial support (and often volunteer labor). Their workplaces or small businesses in town made contributions, which thanks to the organizations' 501(c)3 status, were tax-deductible. Artist friends were tapped to perform at fundraisers or to create pieces of art that could be auctioned off to raise cash. In contrast, less than 10 percent of grassroots INGOs saw any sort of support from foundations.

Most often, grassroots INGOs turned to familiar techniques of fundraising used by domestic nonprofit organizations. Groups based in cities or that had larger budgets hosted galas; others hosted golf outings, charity races, yard sales, and spaghetti dinners. Some raised funds through the sale of imported coffee or handicrafts, and these efforts often were embedded in personal networks—recall the sister of Natalie, FKT's founder, selling hand-made bracelets to her coworkers at Outback Steakhouse. Grass-roots INGOs generate their revenue from familiar local fund raising repertoires and rely on personal networks rather than the endless cycle of grant applications and contract tenders that fund large international NGOs.

The founders of all five case study organizations turned first to family, friends, and fellow church members for their initial contributions. For Kenya's Tomorrow continues to rely almost exclusively on donations from Natalie's family and friends and from two religious congregations in Michigan with which she is associated. The two founders of the Rwanda Ultrasound Initiative got their early donations from friends and family; some in-kind donations from their workplaces followed, and through personal connections they were able to attract a grant of a few thousand dollars from a private foundation. The first donors to Activate Tanzania included the uncle of Erasto's wife, Kate, and Erasto's American host family from his early days as a student in the United States. Local Lutheran churches also contributed early and remain a steady source of income. I asked leaders of all five case study organizations if they had received *any* donations from strangers who had no apparent connection to the group's leaders; for the Rwanda Ultrasound Initiative, For Kenya's Tomorrow, and Activate Tanzania, the answer was no.[11]

The other two groups have now moved beyond their founders' personal networks, but that was where support for both began. Indego Africa was launched with help from Matt Mitro's father and other friends of the family. Its revenue model was to finance the program with the fair-trade style sale of crafts, and those sales have now been supplemented with grants and with contributions from national fundraising events. Wellsprings of Hope began with contributions from Bill Smith's Baptist church. Over the course of several years, members of the Methodist church in the town became involved, and friends, family, and neighbors of those church members began to give for mission trips or sponsor children.

These friends and family gain the satisfaction of helping their loved ones pursue projects that are their passion. For the founders of Indego Africa, For Kenya's Tomorrow, and Activate Tanzania, launching the NGO was a passion project, and the associates I interviewed spoke of offering support for the project because of love and admiration for the founder. One of the board members of For Kenya's Tomorrow, a childhood friend of Natalie, said, "it was important to Natalie, so it was important to me."[12]

Because they are approaching family and friends, leaders' techniques for making the "ask" are old-fashioned. The leaders of For Kenya's Tomorrow, Activate Tanzania, and Indego Africa all started with letters or emails sent out en masse to loved ones. (The tone and format of the letter was also shaped by the writer's previous experience. Natalie's fundraising letter followed the format of letters of solicitation from missionaries. Matt Mitro's first email resembled a business proposal. Headings in the email included several questions: "What is the exact form that this project would take?" "What kind of challenges would we face?" "Will I be reimbursed or compensated?" "What skills is our organization looking for?") Grassroots INGO leaders spoke about their projects at church meetings and book clubs; they went to Rotary meetings and chatted up their neighbors on the street. They asked fellow workers to contribute to their travel or to buy African crafts or come to a fundraiser in a church hall.

Grassroots INGO leaders also rely on their personal networks to recruit volunteers for both domestic tasks and international work. Natalie found short-term "missions teams" to come to Kawangare through her childhood church. Erasto found new board members through his initial contact at a Lutheran Church in St. Paul—the pastor there brought his daughter and son-in-law on board, and the daughter in turn recruited Leann, an elementary school teacher. Since the Rwanda Ultrasound Initiative depends on the specialized medical skills of volunteers, professional networks were more important to them; their medical teams were recruited through hospitals and email lists of professional societies dedicated to emergency medicine.

Relying on personal networks for an organization's material support has several advantages. First, as we have seen, supporters are highly motivated because of their personal trust in and affection for the groups' leaders. These supporters feel that they have a personal stake in the organizations' projects. This sense of personal connection and investment is something that large NGOs try to generate for their donors, even at great expense.[13] For instance, child sponsorship programs put an individual face on donations' recipients, and customized "partnership" programs set up by World Vision make connections between aid recipients and US congregations.[14]

Yet relying on US friends and family for material support also creates difficulties. One volunteer from Wellsprings of Hope, for instance, spoke of her family member's resistance to sponsor a child, and her frustration with herself, believing that she had not done enough to gain support for the cause: "So none of my—my family doesn't sponsor. They pray for me. They know I'm active. . . . I feel like since I've been so frustrated that I haven't been a good enough witness or something."

Volunteers face great frustration when their passions are not met with financial support from their loved ones. Even when these friends and family do give support, the ceiling on potential revenue is low. Leaders' next step is typically to look to organizations within their networks—religious congregations, businesses, community groups—that can make larger donations. This strategy has worked well for Activate Tanzania, Wellsprings of Hope, and For Kenya's Tomorrow; each receives several thousand dollars a year in donations, plus volunteer labor, from churches. Still, these groups fear donor fatigue. The Wellsprings of Hope volunteer illustrated the strain on relationships that this financial dependency can take. Organizational donors can grow weary, too; a second Wellsprings of Hope volunteer said that there is occasional grumbling by his congregation that missions funds go to Wellsprings year after year rather than to other international projects associated with their religious denomination.

Thus, while grassroots INGOs fret about donor fatigue, they also recognize that taking grant or contract funds would impose constraints and administrative burdens. Natalie is reluctant to relinquish her autonomy, while a Wellsprings leader talked about the change in the "relationships" that would happen if Wellsprings expanded and took on professional staff. Leaders point to income-generating activities or local revenue as the middle way that would keep the organizations afloat without compromising relationships. Indego has come closest with its fair-trade-style sales. FKT hopes that the sale of goods from its women's workshop can support programs, while Activate Tanzania is trying to cultivate philanthropy among middle-class Tanzanians. Wellsprings has set up a farm and a brick-making operation to generate cash and supply food to its school. The leaders and supporters are excited about these prospects, which align with the contemporary trend in the nonprofit sector of moving toward social entrepreneurship or "hybrid" organizations. But, to date, these income-generating activities only comprise a small fraction of the groups' revenue. The majority of resources still come from traditional fundraising.

By relying mainly on family and friends for resources, however, grassroots INGOs face little pressure to formally measure their success or account for their spending. Mainstream NGOs are bound by donor agencies' requirements for monitoring, evaluation, and accounting—and the specific standards for these often vary by agency, so NGOs spend more money on accounting than comparably sized multinational corporations.[15] Both their small size and the lack of reporting requirements imposed by donors or their own boards of directors keep grassroots INGOs' administrative burden low. Only Indego Africa, the largest of the case study groups, publishes an annual report. This is not to say that grassroots INGOs do not operate in a spirit of transparency—the groups periodically share figures for how much money they raised at a given event, or how much particular projects cost. More often, they maintain the trust and goodwill of their supporters through personal communications that report on the progress of the projects. The critical difference between grassroots INGOs and larger counterparts is whether accountability to donors is formal or relational.

Relationships with Brokers and Downward Accountability

Blue Marble Dreams might be the only grassroots INGO to come from a relationship forged at the Sundance Institute, but personal relationships that span the United States and the Global South are the seed of most grassroots INGOs. These friends in the aid-receiving communities often become *brokers*—nationals of aid-receiving countries who serve as intermediaries between beneficiaries and donors.[16] Brokers serve as critical links in aid programs (including those funded with millions of dollars through a long aid chain) and in many ways play the most critical role in those chains: they are the ones that do the work of translating donor visions of development into action on the ground. In grassroots INGOs, these broker roles have a special twist; often a friend or relative of the American who started the organization serves as the broker. The groups rely on these brokers not just to get the work done, but to be the channel for downward accountability between the organization and beneficiary communities.

For grassroots INGO leaders, involving friends and relatives in NGO work can also be a practical decision, driven by the need for a trusted agent abroad. In her study of aid projects in Malawi, Ann Swidler observes the practical value of brokers: "[I]n case after case, the critical breakthrough for an NGO is finding the right intermediary, someone who is familiar with the local region and can navigate local barriers for the NGO, but also someone the NGO workers can trust—someone who seems genuinely dedicated to the welfare of the community, who is honest, and who can serve as an extension of the norms of participation and local involvement that the NGO shares."[17] The need for a trusted person-on-the-ground is acute for NGOs with no permanent expatriate staff. Brokers serve not only as literal translators, working between English and local languages, but as cultural translators that adapt American ideas to local realities.[18] Swidler and Watkins, for example, observe how brokers translate the goals of foreign-funded HIV-prevention NGOs to themes that are acceptable to Malawians: fighting stigma and aiding vulnerable women and children.[19] In the case of For Kenya's Tomorrow, Natalie's initial interest in doing something with HIV or orphans in Kenya was translated into week-end children's programs at a church and building latrines in a slum neighborhood.

Brokers who can pull off this translation are typically elites within their communities. In capital cities, "elite" might refer to holders of a PhD, while in rural areas, an elite might be a young man who has completed enough school to write a few paragraphs in the national language. The brokers of grassroots INGOs fall between the bottom and the middle of this spectrum—what Swidler and Watkins call "interstitial elites." In poor communities, these brokers are seen as educated and trustworthy. Crucially, they speak enough English and are connected to global culture through religion, social media, or tourist sites, so they are able to establish relationships with foreigners. By collaborating with foreign NGOs, they stand to reap personal gains that include steady employment and opportunities to travel. Swidler and Watkins also show in their work that interstitial elites who work with aid projects seek something more elusive: a modern identity. Interviews with young adults gaining a toehold in the aid world revealed that they savored not only the material advantages of paid NGO work, but the status of being a white-collar worker, possessing formalized knowledge, and having connections to the cosmopolitan world beyond the village.[20] The hope for a modern, cosmopolitan identity points to why grassroots INGOs are attractive to potential brokers even if they offer limited financial gains. There is abundant opportunity to create relationships with foreigners and to join a globalized social circle. For the pastors of Wellsprings of Hope, there are opportunities to enjoy exchange with foreign visitors, plus increased professional opportunities. The local broker for RUI enjoys the status of being affiliated with a foreign NGO and with doctors from prestigious American hospitals. And as Swidler and Watkins have pointed out, brokers often make these connections never knowing how they might lead to a windfall. In the case of For Kenya's Tomorrow, the broker ended up as the mother-in-law of the group's American founder.

In return, brokers play two important roles for grassroots INGOs. First, these trusted intermediaries oversee most of the groups' on-the-ground work while their American volunteers are back home. In practical terms this can mean the procurement of construction materials, the supervision of laborers, and the preparation of lodging and transportation for visiting American volunteers. These are unglamorous, everyday tasks that require a physical presence in NGO worksites—and knowledge of local languages, prices, and geography. Brokers bring a sort of street smarts, like knowing the fair price to pay for concrete blocks, as well as the social connections that allow them to mobilize people. It often falls to brokers to make the right contacts within government agencies or to bring community members out for meetings.

Second, brokers play an important relational role as "significant others" with whom, and through whom, Americans create emotional bonds with locals. The relationships between Americans and these significant others often predate the creation of the grassroots INGO. The groups' websites are replete with stories of serendipitous meetings between Americans and local people that inspire the Americans to launch an aid project. (The account of Blue Marble Dreams at the beginning of the book is a prime example.) Other relationships are the result not of chance encounters, but of mutual religious networks, as I describe in a later chapter, or through a shared vocation, as was the case with the Rwanda Ultrasound Initiative.

Both the emotional value of the relationship and the local expertise can obscure for grassroots INGO leaders the principal-agent relationship between NGO and broker. Because brokers are viewed as members of the aid-receiving community—and therefore to have aligning interests—and because of the trust and affection between Americans and the brokers, grassroots INGO leaders may assume that the broker can provide downward accountability between Americans and the aid-receiving community. Examples from Wellsprings of Hope, Activate Tanzania, and For Kenya's Tomorrow show how personal relationships are critical to the groups— especially in the founding phases. Personal relationships often evolve into relationships of brokerage, and while these relationships serve practical and emotional goals, they also create strains.

Brokerage Relationships in the Case Study Organizations

For Erasto, the founder of Activate Tanzania, the relationship is with his family and friends of his hometown. Muyinga is a village of about two thousand people; his mother remains there, along with some of his younger siblings. Erasto periodically sent cash to relatives and friends after he immigrated to the United States. While this satisfied his relatives, Erasto became more unsatisfied— he felt that remittances would never make his family self-reliant. In his telling, Erasto's idea of a broader gift always centered on the village. Erasto and Kate's plan for a school soon involved a cousin of Erasto's, who lived part-time in the village, and a childhood friend born in the village but then living in a city. In the years since, the two men have remained stalwarts of the school. One is the school's administrator, Erasto's right-hand man-on-the-ground, while the other is the school's longest-serving teacher.

Erasto's labors over the last decade have been extraordinary. He estimates that he spends ten to twenty hours a week dealing with school business, and his organization has raised hundreds of thousands of dollars. In the setup phase of the school, Erasto's cousin was the crucial broker, and Erasto told me, "To be honest, if it wasn't for him, I don't think the school would be [there]." The benefits of their labor for the village are what Erasto envisioned— an excellent secondary school, whose nearest match in quality is more than thirty kilometers away in the regional capital. The village has also benefitted from the ten full-tuition scholarships for village students that the Activate board promised in exchange for title to the school's land. Muyinga further profits from the presence of more than a hundred students and teachers, who buy sundries in village shops; provide business for the mini-bus drivers shuttling to the regional capital and back; and hire local cooks, groundskeepers, and laundresses.

To manage this huge enterprise, and to balance the desires and demands of Tanzanian family, friends, and former neighbors on one hand, and American in-laws, friends, fellow-congregants, and donors on the other, requires tremendous interpersonal and emotional work from Erasto. Activate Tanzania volunteer Leann acknowledged the strain Erasto faces between fellow Tanzanians, who have expectations of what the village is owed or what a private Tanzanian school should look like, and the American board, which has its own notions about pedagogy and budget allocation. For example, the Tanzanian teachers were pressing for more classroom space. The American board noted that the school's dining hall provided ample seating—why not teach classes there outside of meal times? Erasto had to convey to the board the practical and cultural issues around food preparation in rural Tanzania— cooking meals is an hours-long affair involving open pots over wood fires—and simply buying gas stoves, as some board members suggested, would have been alien and badly received. Leann explained of Erasto's position, "I think it's very hard for him. He's so passionate about doing this stuff there, and he gets the information and then provides it for the board here and a lot of times it's not received well because it's not the American way. And so he's caught in that middle all the time. . . . And it's very heart wrenching, I know, for him." The strong personal relationships Erasto has in Muyinga create strain between being a good "hometown boy" and an effective chair of an American board of directors.

The work of For Kenya's Tomorrow has been defined by the relationship of its founder, Natalie, to her Kenyan husband, David, and by extension to David's mother, Ruth, and to his childhood friend, Martin. Ruth, a pastor of a small Pentecostal church, was one of Natalie's early contacts in the slum neighborhood of Kawangare. Natalie describes meeting Ruth as a case of divine intervention. Natalie had encountered Ruth twice at church, and felt led by God to approach her:

> I went up to her afterwards and I said, "I don't know if this is gonna make sense to you or if this is something you're even gonna want to do, but I really—I've been praying that God would provide somebody that I can be mentored by, and I really feel like it's you." And she looked at me and she said, "Absolutely, I've been waiting for you for the last year." And she had had a vision the year prior of this white girl coming to her saying that. . . . And so she was ready for it, like her heart was already in line with it.

Natalie's partnership with Ruth's church gained her trust in the neighborhood and local cooperation. Natalie soon began dating David, Ruth's son, and after their marriage David became a full partner in FKT's work. The area around Ruth's church became the base of the NGO's projects—street cleanups, a Saturday morning program for children, and latrines. Martin also became a critical partner. He owned a van and had started his own business to transport tourists around Kenya's national parks; soon, he became the designated driver for FKT's work and several times a year took American volunteers to Maasai Mara park for a backcountry experience. His parents owned a tract of land in Kawangare that they sold to FKT as a site for the women's craft workshop. When David and Natalie were in the United States, Martin supervised the craft workshop and served as FKT's general man-on-the-ground.

A friendship was also at the genesis of Wellsprings of Hope. As I described in chapter 1, Wellsprings began after Pastor Bill Smith visited Uganda with a delegation of Baptist preachers, and the initial goal was to provide financial support for the "ministry" of five Ugandan pastors that he met there. Bill spoke in emotional terms about a week of itinerant preaching with the Ugandan pastors, camping in the bush, and their initial discussions about the organization they would launch together. With tears, he told me: "That week—because those are my best friends in the whole world, those men. All of them are still living. . . . I've wondered what it's gonna be like when one of them goes to be with the Lord. But, anyway, it's a big deal to me because as they shared their vision, God allowed me to get in on it." He went on to explain how that relationship trumped existing patterns of religious assistance—namely, why he decided to launch his own organization and fund these pastors rather than supporting existing NGOs or Southern Baptist missionaries. "Well, brought up as a Southern Baptist, that was my paradigm. . . . We'll send money to mission organizations that do this kind of work. But when we went, we ate with these people. And the answer is, it became a relationship, and it was no longer a middle-man, we were having fun partnering with them directly. And so, you know, maybe somebody else could—and maybe it was rein-venting the wheel, but, man, it was our wheel."

Those five pastors became the administrators of the multi-project grassroots INGO: in addition to their congregations, they established two schools, two clinics, men's and women's Bible classes, a farm, and a child sponsorship program. The pastors are paid a monthly sal-ary, which has brought them to middle-class standing; all own houses, and one has a car. Noting the pastors' increasing weight, Bill told them, only half in jest, "You know, you guys are starting to look more and more like Americans; that's not a good thing."

These three grassroots INGOs were built around personal rela-tionships, but they were designed as organizations that would have broader public benefits than individual remittances. Erasto's rela-tionships in Muyinga bore fruit for the students and residents there more broadly. All the residents who worked in FKT's craft shop, attended the children's program, or used the public toilets in Kawangare profited from Natalie's personal commitments to peo-ple who lived in that neighborhood. What could have been a pro-gram by Wellsprings to subsidize the salaries of pastors in Uganda instead was designed as a regional network of churches, clinics, and schools.

In each of these cases, private benefits also accrued to the African brokers in the relationship. They often gained steady employment, increased business, status, and a reliable middle-class salary. Erasto's old friends took positions at the school. Ruth's church saw an inflow of resources, while Martin's tour business gained built-in customers; the pastors effectively became, in addi-tion to religious leaders, nonprofit executives.

But these private benefits for friends and family were not intended as rents. Americans saw these roles for African friends as necessary for the smooth operation of the organization. All of the groups required local brokers to execute their projects, and these friends and family members served as trusted agents. Grassroots INGOs are particularly dependent on these brokers, because the organizations' leaders spend little time in the receiving country. And unlike larger NGOs, there are few codified procedures for administering projects or handling money. They do not rely on the professional management techniques that permeate large international NGOs.[21] Rather, grassroots INGOs depend on their trusted local partners to execute the projects.

This system has its failures. The embezzling of thousands of dollars by one of Bill's Ugandan "best friends" is one example. Activate Tanzania found its school threatened when a former neighbor of Erasto's, an aspiring politician, tried to claim ownership of the school for the village. Erasto had to dispatch a lawyer to the regional capital to demonstrate the claim of the Activate board to the school property. The episode left a bitter aftertaste in the village, with some residents feeling that the school had become "in" the village, but not "of" it; tuition and entrance standards had risen such that some children of secondary-school age in the village could not attend, and instead went to the inferior public school nearby.

These misadventures show how grassroots INGOs' problems of accountably are rooted in the structure of their relationships. Writing about the accountability of Northern and Southern NGOs, Alnoor Ebrahim argues, "Accountability is a relational concept. It does not stand objectively apart from organizational relationships, since the demands for accountability and the mechanisms used to achieve it are constructed by those very relationships."[22] The weak local knowledge of most grassroots INGO leaders and the strong emotional ties they have with their brokers are the critical factors in shaping their downward accountability. Grassroots INGO leaders—even those born in the aid-receiving country, like Erasto—are strongly dependent on their brokers to be their agents to execute projects. But these brokers remain principals in their *own* lives and family networks. Swidler and Watkins remind us that African social relations are guided by logics of patronage: NGOs are patrons to brokers, but brokers, in turn, are regarded as patrons by their friends and family. To be a good family member is to look out for the interests of relatives, and to channel resources downward.[23] Just as Erasto was viewed as a patron by his relatives, now his brokers, with their salaries provided by the school, are seen as patrons by their dependents.

The close emotional bond between American leaders and the brokers can create awkwardness as brokers try to manage their roles as principal and agent. The American leaders recognize the separate interests of their brokers, and want to offer them benefits. As the partners with greater financial power they are in the difficult position of deciding how much to offer these brokers who are dear friends, cousins, or even mothers-in-law. They have to take into account the demands placed on one another by their personal relationships. But as leaders of organizations funded by donations, the grassroots INGO leaders must also ensure that their spending is fair and reasonable by local standards. Bill and the fellow American Wellsprings leaders, for example, were initially uneasy about a minivan instead of motorbikes for the pastors to use. And, in the absence of institutional knowledge or peer organizations that can tell them what is fair and reasonable, who do American leaders rely on to learn what is fair and reasonable? The brokers. The Ugandan pastors explained that the minivan would be useful for transporting ill students or parishioners, or hauling supplies from one site to another. And, according to local customs, the minivan could be parked at one of the pastor's houses in the evening rather than at the office. Until the embezzling crisis, Wellsprings of Hope had faith in—or less charitably, ignored—its brokers' handling of its principal-agent conflicts of interest.

Downward accountability points to a *third* role that brokers play. Because of their limited social networks, language skills, and time in the field, the American leaders of grassroots INGOs often count on the brokers to speak on behalf of the beneficiary communities. They become the *community's* unelected agents. In lieu of more robust mechanisms of participation, often it is the brokers who suggest appropriate projects or represent concerns to the Americans. Wellsprings' annual priority-setting meeting involves the five Ugandan pastors and the American board. Yet what we know about brokers suggests that this is hardly an ideal structure for downward accountability. These brokers are already in the position of principal for themselves and agent for the grassroots INGO. Moreover, they are not representative of the community in meaningful ways; they are often more educated, more cosmopolitan, and wealthier; they are usually men.

Grassroots INGOs can reduce their dependence on brokers for downward accountability. Indego has done this by creating partnerships with existing Rwandan cooperatives rather than serving individual artisans. The cooperatives have their own elected leadership, and they can deliberate independently and decide if they are satisfied and want to maintain their partnership with Indego. Activate Tanzania has set up a school board of directors in Muyinga to assess the needs of the school in context. These directors can better monitor regulations from the Ministry of Education, the conditions of the school, and relationships between the school and the residents of Muyinga. Whether by creating bodies for downward accountability or engaging existing local ones, partnerships like these move grassroots INGOs a step away from a model based on personal relationships and emotional bonds. Creating such partnerships may not be simple if Americans are on site for only weeks of the year; but since grassroots INGOs typically invest in one place for a long period of time rather than looking for a quick exit or replication, they have more potential to build the partnerships than do other NGOs.

If grassroots INGOs create broader relationships with the communities they aid, downward accountability can be richer. Ebrahim describes a version of accountability that is more than bean counting. Rather than a process by which one body controls another, accountability can be an "enabling process" where the organization and its proxies "develop congruent interests and missions."[24] Fry argues that meaningful accountability is less about creating systems to identify and punish deviations from the norms than about creating the shared norms themselves.[25] A grassroots INGO that wanted to operate this way would need to seek out broader feedback, have regular and sustained dialogue about past successes and failures and future priorities, and be willing to depart from the preferences and assumptions of American volunteers. This demands that grassroots INGO leaders take a step away from aid as a "personal project." Yet it is consistent with the relational goals of many grassroots INGO leaders, if they have the time and patience to engage.

· · ·

Grassroots INGOs are upwardly accountable to governments, in a minimal sense, and have only loose accountability to their donors. Larger NGOs are constantly pushed to demonstrate their results and to create projects that can be replicated. Grassroots INGOs, since they are supported by personal networks of family and friends, are immune to these pressures. Their accountability to their donors is relational rather than formal. This gives grassroots INGOs an opportunity to do the sorts of projects that are out of fashion with donors, or to engage in work that is important but that is slow or is difficult to measure for a report.

I have argued that grassroots INGOs are defined by the personal relationships between Americans and people in the Global South, and that the principal-agent relationship is often layered over ties of friendly or intimate relationships. This approach reduces some sources of uncertainty. It allows the Americans, in the absence of a more comprehensive political or social scientific analysis, to identify recipients and projects. It provides them with trusted on-the-ground knowledge, including knowledge of local languages and customs. But brokers are put in the compromised position of having to simultaneously represent their private interests, the interests of the NGO, and the interests of the local community they are thought to represent. Grassroots INGOs can move toward richer forms of accountability by relying less on brokers and creating or engaging with local collectivities that can provide independent feedback.

If the relational structure of grassroots INGOs shapes their accountabilities, it also shapes their influence in the United States. In the next chapter I turn to the ways that these groups shape the everyday Americans' imaginations about the Global South.

6   Seen It with Their Own Eyes

Grassroots INGOs' Discourse

Activate Tanzania's first major fundraising event was a benefit dinner called "Come to Afrika." A drumming group performed as guests circulated around the hall of a suburban Lutheran church, shopping for Tanzanian handicrafts and sampling pan-African dishes. Activate's founders chose not to make this a political event, framing the lack of education in Muyinga as unjust or a violation of human rights; instead, they took a page from the established fundraising playbook for schools, libraries, and other cultural institutions. At the event they held, Muyinga—Tanzania—Africa was portrayed as someplace vaguely exotic, warm, and inviting. It was a place where an American now had an opportunity to build something, to invest. The image given was one of long-term growth and reliability, where donors could make a contribution that was sure to do good.

If money is what flows in from American friends to grassroots INGOs, what flows back is no less important: ways of understanding poverty, development, and the aid-receiving countries themselves. The accounts of grassroots INGO leaders provide a lens through which other Americans see developing countries. Organizations' written materials are one crucial source of these accounts. We've seen that websites emphasize heroic individuals as the agents of change. Volunteers are portrayed as transforming the lives of aid recipients and themselves. The recipients are typically depicted suffering or as hardworking, ambitious individuals. The institutions in developing countries that are brought into view for American audiences are most often NGOs or religious congregations; government makes the occasional cameo appearance to support a project but is also spoken of as an impediment to real change.

Aid organizations of all sizes have websites and other digital means to broadcast their ideas to an anonymous public. Returning to the case studies allows us to see what is unique about grassroots INGOs' ability to frame their ideas. It is the interpersonal instances of framing distinctive to grassroots INGOs that I want to emphasize in this chapter, rather than the broadcasted ones. I argue that these moments of framing are especially powerful because of the relational influence between speaker and listener, and because many listeners have scant knowledge of the Global South. Every conversation about a trip to Africa and every fundraising pitch is an occasion for grassroots INGOs to frame development problems and articulate Americans' role in solving them. (In the next chapter I give special attention to religious forms of framing.) Because of their deep personal networks in American communities, grassroots INGOs have the ability to shape American perceptions in the same way that missionaries and returning Peace Corps volunteers have in generations past.

But these grassroots INGOs work in an era where much more thought has been given to how accounts of people in developing countries matter. In the next pages I consider some of the effects of NGOs' power to shape everyday citizens' ideas—the power of discourse—and describe mainstream INGOs' recent efforts to grapple with that power. Examples from Activate Tanzania and Wellsprings of Hope show how the people most intimately involved in grassroots INGOs condense the complex realities they encounter in developing countries into messages that can be shared with their families and friends. After showing how these volunteers share these messages—in their work, through their churches, and occasionally on bigger stages—I argue that the discourse of grassroots INGOs is apt to be especially influential, but also biased.

NGOs and the Power of Discourse

Grassroots international NGOs offer Americans particular lenses on the Global South and on questions of poverty, inequality, and development. I showed in chapter 3 that these groups present development on a human scale; complex political and economic problems become the individual quests for a "great escape." I argue here that grassroots INGOs are important because of the power they have to frame distant people and problems for listeners. Organizations' leaders encounter complex social arrangements that must be made into legible problems that can be solved with donors' action. Grassroots INGOs create ways of understanding developing countries for their supporters with the images they share, the stories they tell, the virtues they praise, and the deficits they raise money to fill. This ability to create a lens that shapes others' vision is the power of discourse.

Discourse, according to Dryzek and Niemeyer, is a set of categories and concepts that allows individuals to "process sensory inputs into coherent accounts, which can then be shared in intersubjectively meaningful fashion."[1] This process of making mental order out of chaos is ubiquitous in human life. Its *political* dimension is the way sets of categories circulate among people and constrain other ways of thinking, often reinforcing or challenging relations of power. When grassroots INGO leaders make the case for their projects to fellow Americans, the discourse they use privileges a certain definition of a situation while occluding others. As Dryzek and Niemeyer explain, "Discourses enable as well as constrain thought, speech, and action. Any discourse embodies some conception of common sense and acceptable knowledge; it may embody power by recognizing some interests as valid while repressing others."[2]

In her treatise on the political ethics of humanitarian INGOs, Jennifer Rubenstein argues that one of INGOs' defining qualities—and a trait that makes INGO work inherently political—is that they use discourse to shape the public's perception of developing countries.[3] She argues that INGO discourse has tended to emphasize the suffering and minimize the agency of people in aid-receiving countries. Discourse centered on suffering and the power of INGOs to alleviate it skews perceptions of aid-receiving countries, encourages paternalism, and rallies support for counterproductive aid interventions. She writes, "For example, a close-up photograph of a wide-eyed, dejected child . . . will likely leave viewers who lack other reliable sources of information about these issues with the (usually) mistaken impression that the child's suffering is fundamentally due to a lack of material resources, that she has no family or community to care for her, and/or that she needs an outsider to "'save'" her, perhaps by sending food or shoes."[4]

Just as importantly, such discourse can obscure other understandings of aid-receiving countries and discourage other ways of understanding inequality. She argues that there are practical consequences: these ways of thinking about developing countries can discourage foreign investment and tourism. They can obscure for people in rich countries the roles of agricultural subsidies, trade agreements, and climate change—things over which their own governments have influence—in the ability of people in poor countries to make sustainable livings.

Large INGOs have grappled with their discursive power, particularly how the images in their fundraising materials shape public perceptions. The American Red Cross used graphic images of suffering in its fundraising materials as early as World War I.[5] The images of listless, dark-skinned people—usually women and children—became a trope of INGO fundraising in the second half of the twentieth century. Lamers notes that these portrayals are effective both because of their pathos and because children are almost universally cast as *deserving* poor—they cannot be at fault for their misfortune.[6]

Representations of suffering in the Global South spiked during the Ethiopian famine of 1983–84, when news broadcasts and INGO appeals brought images of malnourished African children with distended bellies into American living rooms on a nightly basis.[7] INGOs faced a wave of criticism that such images amounted to "poverty pornography."[8] By portraying only images of destitution and helplessness, critics argued, such photographs "reinforce already widespread perceptions of cultural and intellectual superiority among Northern publics, as well as the belief that benevolent donors in the North are the primary source of solutions for the 'problems' of the South."[9] Many development INGOs have subsequently shifted their publicity tactics, their discourse emphasizing instead empowerment of aid recipients or the cosmopolitanism of Northern donors.[10]

If it is unavoidable that INGOs will shape their donors' perceptions, INGOs can shape their discourse in ways that are less likely to stereotype aid recipients, to encourage paternalism, or to black-box structural causes of global inequalities. Rubenstein argues that discourse can do "real harm . . . by limiting people's capacity for critical reflection." For her, the normative test for discursive power is whether the discourse "make[s] it more difficult for others to critically examine and—if they so choose—revise their own perceptions and assumptions."[11] Does INGO discourse give room for aid recipients to speak? Does it permit conflict? Or does it restrict the voices of others? Does it use our experiences and preferences as proxies for those of aid recipients?

Evaluating discourse by this standard requires attention to the social context. Rubenstein rightly argues that INGO discourse has less influence on donors' understanding of disasters that donors have personal familiarity with—earthquakes and tornadoes—than they do with famine and severe poverty.[12] She claims that INGO discourse increases in power when the social distance between donor and recipient is great, and when there are few alternative sources of information.

The discourse of grassroots INGOs fits this profile. Grassroots INGOs have smaller audiences than do mainstream aid organizations, but for those audiences, two of grassroots INGOs' features give their discourse the potential to be especially salient. First, the discourse of grassroots INGO leaders is apt to be especially influential because of personal trust between leaders and supporters. As we have seen, nearly all of the material support comes from groups' leaders' personal networks—family members, coworkers, or friends. American supporters of grassroots INGOs trust the accounts of these close associates. When leaders claim personal knowledge of a problem, having "seen it with their own eyes," their accounts powerfully shape the thinking of their friends and family.

The second difference between mainstream INGOs' and grassroots INGOs' discourse is the particularism and episodic relationship with the aid-receiving country that characterizes the latter's work. The concepts and categories that can be conveyed by grassroots INGOs are limited from the outset by their leaders' limited language skills, their constrained geographic exposure, and their selection into projects that appeal to them. As we saw in chapter 3, grassroots INGO leaders typically make sense of development with reference to their vocational skills or their families' histories of economic mobility. The possibilities about what can be conveyed about an aid-receiving country by grass-roots INGO leaders to fellow Americans are constrained by the leaders' very limited knowledge and the lack of settings (formal education or professional networks) for those leaders to reflect on those limits.

Building on what we've seen from grassroots INGOs' websites about the discourse itself and the partner organizations through which they transmit it, in the next section I present two extended examples from the case studies. These examples show in finer detail the ways in which grassroots INGO leaders' own experiences and values shape the lens through which they view poverty. They further show how discourse is transmitted through personal net-works of families, colleagues, and congregants, shaping how those people come to understand problems in the Global South and Americans' potential to help.

Africa through the Lens of Activate Tanzania: Poor in Money, Rich in Community

Leann, the volunteer for Activate Tanzania, has provided a lens on Africa through her personal and professional relationships. She is an elementary school teacher in the suburbs of St. Paul, Minnesota. When I interviewed her, she had made two trips of several weeks to Tanzania to volunteer at Activate's secondary school. Her work there entailed assisting with the English-language classes and running professional development workshops for the Tanzanian faculty. But, just as one of the three objectives of Peace Corps volunteers is to bring knowledge of foreign countries to Americans, so Leann felt that teaching Americans about Tanzania was a critical part of her service with the NGO.

She invited me to visit her classroom in the first weeks of the school year. On the walls and shelves of the room were African, Asian, and Latin American textiles, curios, and dolls, as well as several illustrations of the word *ujamaa*, a Swahili term that translates roughly as "community," "brotherhood," or "fellowship." After I had observed the class for some time, Leann told the children I would be traveling to Tanzania soon and asked them to share what they had learned about the place in those first weeks of school. One student raised a hand and said that people there are very poor but the children are good at creating their own toys out of materials on hand. (Makeshift soccer balls made of plastic bags and twine were among the souvenirs in the classroom.) Yes, Leann asked, but what are they rich in? *Ujamaa*, the class answered. In Tanzania people are poor in money but they are rich in community.

In our interview later that day, Leann explained to me that she taught about Tanzania to develop empathy among her students:

"I do intentionally show them toys or show them tools because I want them to understand they're just like you. They're like you even though they're in a different part of the world; they have different tools, but they're like you and . . . to make this place a better place, we need to have tolerance for each other." Her lessons emphasized shared humanity and respect: "Just because you don't have something, doesn't mean you're not rich." At the same time, the lessons in "giving back" had to do with sharing material wealth. For holiday celebrations students would bring in donations for Heifer International, Feed My Starving Children (an emergency food aid charity), or for a program for care packages for deployed US soldiers. Leann had begun integrating lessons about Tanzania into her teaching several years earlier, so by the date of our interview, two hundred students— between twenty-four and twenty-eight a year—had learned about Tanzania through the lens of Leann's work with the NGO.

Leann's work with Activate Tanzania aligned with critical parts of her self-identity: as a worldly, unprejudiced person, and her vocation as a teacher. During our interview her eyes teared up as she discussed the Minnesota community where she grew up. "[It] was not very diverse at all and I saw a lot of prejudice. . . . I see now it was uneducated prejudice." She saw sharing her work with Activate Tanzania and raising money as an opportunity to reach out to family and former neighbors: "So I'm gonna write uneducated family members, uneducated community members, educators who we learned some of the negative things [from] as well as the positive things." She believes that her work has "had an impact" on her family. "They see the world as a much smaller place where perhaps they can help out."

Perhaps the most consequential contact of Leann's was Evan, her former student teacher, who came to volunteer at the secondary school in Muyinga for six months. During his visit, several leaders invited Evan for lunch and made a bold request: that he help them raise money for a preschool. Evan agreed. When he returned to the United States, he registered his own NGO and began raising money as he worked on and off at his family's Minneapolis liquor store. The store was a regular contributor to community events, but now their donations and the cash from annual golf outings went to build the preschool in Muyinga. Evan raised enough money to build three classrooms. When I met him two years later, he had not been back to Tanzania—he asked me to take some pictures of the classrooms his family's money had built when I visited.

Leann understood the lessons to her students as being about empathy and "giving back." The other lesson that was carried by Leann and Evan was about the place of education in Tanzania's development. The name of Evan's NGO (which I omit here to preserve his anonymity) conjured an image of Tanzanian children gathering around kerosene lamps at night to study. This was what Evan had seen in Muyinga, and the message he wanted to send his friends was about the desire of Tanzanians to learn and the difficulties they faced in doing so. This message was carried through beer-fueled golf outings, church youth group meetings, letters to elderly aunts in rural Minnesota, and classrooms full of American elementary school children. In describing what she'd seen in Tanzania that she wanted to convey to her American students, Leann said: "Education's my passion, and I believe that the people in Tanzania value that. And not value it because I want them to value it. . . . Because I've been there and I've seen that, I think I can show them [my students] kids who are hungry for an education."

I want to emphasize two things about how this education lens is created by someone like Leann. First, she said, "Education's my passion." In our interview Leann revealed that she had a long history of volunteering for various causes, but her trip to Tanzania with Activate was her first travel abroad. She chose an organization that aligned with her vocational skills and what she called her "passion." What she came to see as a critical problem in Tanzania was limited by the issues that were important to her. Second, she said, "I've been there and I've seen that." Her faith in Tanzanians' need and desire for education comes from the fact that she traveled there, and as she said, saw it for herself. Her assessment of the needs and desires of Tanzanians came not from social scientific theories of development or of broad travel and assessment of Tanzania's social services. It was based on what she saw with her own eyes on a trip for a project she chose. Her interests or "passion" became the basis for an image of distant people and their problems that was shared with many other Americans through personal networks. Her ideas were transmitted to students over whom she had authority, colleagues over whom she had influence, and elder kin and neighbors whom she hoped to affect.

Africa through Wellsprings of Hope: "I've Got a Big God."

Every volunteer for Wellsprings of Hope knows the story of Lindsey, a nine-year-old girl who raised $25,000 to build a classroom in Uganda. Lindsey and her mother learned about Wellsprings of Hope in 2010 through a chance conversation with a fellow volunteer en route to a project feeding homeless people in San Antonio. Soon after, Lindsey read a children's book about a teenage boy who had raised money for people in Africa with AIDS by engaging his classmates in basketball shoot-a-thon. The idea captured Lindsey's imagination. Having just learned about Wellsprings of Hope, and with her mother's encouragement, Lindsey decided to launch her own fundraiser aimed at building a classroom for one of Wellsprings' elementary schools in Uganda. She was able to extract a promise from her parents that if she raised enough money, they would get to travel to Uganda to see the new building. (Her mother told me that she believed that raising the money would be possible, but it would be over the course of several years.)

The fundraiser caught on among the students at Lindsey's private Christian school. A read-a-thon and other fundraisers from the schoolchildren raised half of the sum. More donations came from Lindsey's family and friends, and from members of church and community groups that Lindsey gave talks to about her project. Within five months she had raised $25,000. The board members regarded this donation with surprise and admiration, and soon with the notion that God was working through the young girl. Lindsey's parents made good on their promise and the family of four (including Lindsey's younger sister) traveled to Uganda in spring 2011 for the dedication of the new classroom building. A plaque with Lindsey's name hangs on the building's wall. In the following year, Lindsey was asked to speak to service clubs at Texas A&M and Texas State and was interviewed on a nationally syndicated Christian radio show.

Wellsprings of Hope volunteers tell this story to emphasize God's greatness and a girl's boldness and generosity. But the story also shows the poignancy and effectiveness of an American child raising money for Ugandan children. Lindsey's account of an encounter with a Ugandan girl that her family sponsored illustrates the pathos in the comparison of Ugandan and American children—the former destitute, and the latter surrounded by resources so abundant that they can be diverted to strangers:

And we met in Uganda—there was a girl, she's in third grade and her Dad died when she was young and her Mom is gone days at a time working, so she has to take care of herself. She doesn't really have like food and proper shelter and medical care and all that. And so we decided to sponsor her and we asked, "Is there anything that we can pray with you for?" And she says, "Just pray that I stay alive." And I'm like, "You're in third grade, you should not be worrying about that." When I was in third grade, I did not worry about staying alive.

When Lindsey speaks to college service clubs or church groups, they hear about Uganda as a destitute place where one can encounter a child on the street who fears for her life.

In Lindsey's account, the social and economic conditions of Uganda are reduced to problems of poverty; the problems of poverty are defined as problems of facilities and material provision for children; these problems are defined as a problem of fundraising; the problem of fundraising is defined as a problem of will. Lindsey's account is simplified, as one would expect a child's to be, yet her discourse—and her example—are powerful for American audiences. What is implied by Lindsey's story is that the social and economic conditions of Uganda could be transformed if well-meaning Americans could generate enough will. A child is the ideal exemplar for this theory, because her innocence seems to contrast with the self-serving excuses of adults who could mobilize huge amounts of resources but do not. Lindsey's mother described herself as "realistic" in contrast to her daughter's childish enthusiasm. Recalling Lindsey's notion of raising enough for a school, her mother had thought, "'You're not going to raise $25,000. That's just not reality.' And so I wanted—I didn't want her to be disappointed." But, in this family's religious beliefs, the will to do something involves trusting that God will help bring it to bear. This was Lindsey's response to her mother's doubts: "I've got a big God. He can do anything." Lindsey's donation became a powerful narrative for Wellsprings that illustrated the power of will infused by religious faith.

. . .

These stories give us examples of grassroots INGOs' discourse on poverty and development and illustrate ways that it radiates through supporters' personal networks. The settings in which discourse happens are school classrooms, fundraising events, bus rides to volunteer projects, radio interviews, letters to relatives, and speeches to service clubs. The numbers of people reached through these contacts are smaller than those that mainstream INGOs reach through public relations campaigns, but grassroots INGOs' accounts have special power because the speakers have "seen it with their own eyes." These perspectives are also prone to be influential because they are passed through trusted relationships: between teacher and student, within congregations, among family members. Grassroots INGOs can become causes célèbres in American communities, generating fundraising frenzies that raise tens of thousands of dollars.

The depictions of aid recipients here, like those in grassroots INGO websites, are generally positive. The examples here emphasized shared qualities of humanity and portrayed recipients' ingenuity, work ethic, and hunger for knowledge. Leann even tried to teach her students that poor Tanzanian communities had assets of their own. These are surely improvements over stereotypes of

Africa as the home of famine, corruption, and war. The presence of immigrant leaders of grassroots INGOs also provides new depictions of the Global South for some Americans. Websites suggest that roughly one-third of grassroots INGOs are led by immigrants from the aid-receiving country. The opening vignette of this chapter showed how the "African-ness" in Activate Tanzania was stylized for an American audience, but Erasto himself offers some of Activate's supporters a novel understanding of Africa. By supporting Activate, a number of Minnesotans may have encountered for the first time an African man as a high-tech professional, and as an agent of change in Tanzania rather than an object of it.

But while it rouses Americans' compassion and other good feelings—and while it is sometimes effective in raising cash—grassroots INGOs' discourse is also constrained and constraining. What these volunteers had seen with their own eyes was far more than had their American friends and family, but it wasn't much. Leann's time in Tanzania was several weeks, and Lindsey began her fundraising before setting foot in Uganda. In addition to their short time in those places and their limited language skills, these volunteers experienced a sort of selection effect: they chose to support these programs because of their own skills and interests. The volunteers then went home and portrayed what they saw as an assessment of what Tanzanians or Ugandans needed and wanted. The short-term, personal accounts on which grassroots INGOs are built favor something Rubenstein warned against: substituting givers' own experiences and preferences as proxies for receivers'.

Grassroots INGOs face an intractable problem in helping Americans revise their thinking of the Global South: their discourse cannot be extracted from the aid relationship. No matter how hardworking or virtuous the aid recipient, in grassroots

INGOs' discourse their fate hinges on Americans' willingness to act. This depiction is often more paternalistic than the programs are on the ground. As the last chapter showed, while they sometimes flounder in the attempt, many organizations aim to meaningfully share decision-making with local leaders. But these attempts at partnership are effaced in discourse that puts American agency at the center. Grassroots INGOs' reliance on personal donations means that the stories they tell are shaped by the imperative to raise funds. And the logic of fundraising demands that donors—not beneficiaries—are the heroes of the story.

Rubenstein acknowledges that it is exceedingly difficult for INGOs to talk about their work in ways that challenge Northern stereotypes of the South. What would be ideal, she suggests, "is an institutional context in which a diverse array of differently situated actors, with different experiences, identities, and incentives, contribute to the shaping of shared perceptions."[13] Grassroots INGOs seem to offer promise here because they contribute to organizational plurality, and because personal relationships with aid-receiving communities could offer a platform for Southern actors to offer new perspectives to the United States. The Americans most intimately involved in grassroots INGOs—the founders, like Bill, who had to deal with Wellsprings' near-collapse, or Megan and Tamara, who have had to work cheek-by-jowl with the Rwanda Ministry of Health—develop relationships where there is space for conflict, for recipients of aid to speak. But at each remove the nuance of these relationships is lost and the task of discourse becomes increasingly about drumming up funds, leaving people in the Global South "rich in community" but waiting on American generosity.

7 Networks, Frames, Modes of Action

Roles for Religion

When I founded [For Kenya's Tomorrow] I purposely did not found it as a religious organization for a couple of different reasons. . . . It comes with a certain connotation, I guess you can say. And I didn't want anybody who wanted to come and serve to feel left out. Do you know what I mean? Whether or not you are a Christian or a Muslim, or a Jew or whatever, I wanted it to be an open door for people to come and serve. Not limited to any type of religion. And I also felt, too, like in my conversations with God, that God was just saying to me that there are so many Christian organizations that are out there doing things in my name that aren't a true representation of really who I am. So just lead by example. And that's kind of how I felt about it, too.

Natalie, the thirty-year-old founder of For Kenya's Tomorrow, illustrates the difficulty in designating a grassroots international NGO as religious. Both Natalie and her Kenyan husband are Pentecostals; her mother-in-law is the pastor of the small Nairobi church that is the key partner for aid projects; the bulk of FKT's funding and volunteers come from Natalie's childhood church in Michigan. A recent newsletter punctuates the group's successes with the exclamation "PRAISE JESUS!"

And yet Natalie does not describe For Kenya's Tomorrow as a "faith-based" or "religious" organization. For her, to be a "religious organization" is to restrict volunteering to those who share the same faith. It also suggests that an organization is claiming a divine mandate for its work—"doing things in my name." She fears that Christian groups abuse this mantle, "doing things . . . that aren't a true representation of who I [God] really am." To be more authentically Christian, then, is to eschew the label of "religious" but to "lead by example." For Kenya's Tomorrow defines itself as a secular organization even though religion shapes its programs, its partners, and its leader's decisions.

Consider also the founding of Activate Tanzania. When Erasto and Kate broached the idea of building a school, their friends suggested that Erasto meet with a local Lutheran minister who had traveled several times to Tanzania through a sister-church program. Pastor Dan's church became a dedicated donor to the school, and until the school was legally incorporated as an independent nonprofit its funds were wired through the Saint Paul Area Synod. Why would an immigrant with wholly secular development objectives team up with a Lutheran pastor? And why would an aid group infused with Pentecostalism reject the label of "faith-based?"

The presence of religion in this field of organizations is unmistakable and sometimes emerges in surprising ways. Natalie's narrative above and her explanation of being "led" to work with her mother-in-law's church (described in chapter 5) reflect her belief in divine intervention. Wellsprings of Hope is administered in Uganda by a team of pastors, and I have described how evangelical Christian scripts of confession and forgiveness helped the group navigate a management crisis. Grassroots INGOs' websites indicate religious ties in other ways: by showing a religious symbol such as a cross on the group's homepage (6%); by citing scripture on the website (12%); by naming board members' religious affiliations (26%); or by naming a religious congregation as a partner (43%). As I discussed in chapter 2, websites show that 15 percent of grassroots INGOs have projects that are explicitly religious in nature, such as training clergy, distributing food on religious holidays, raising church buildings, evangelizing, and teaching Bible studies. The majority of religious ties that appear in the sample of 150 organizations are Protestant or Catholic, but connections to Mormon, Muslim, Jewish, Hindu, and Buddhist traditions appear, too. I expect that as further work on grassroots INGOs based in other countries emerges, US-based organizations will be distinctive in part because of religion's significant role.

Yet the effort to label a grassroots INGO as "religious" or "secular" or to determine what share of these groups are "religious" fundamentally misunderstands the nature of these organizations. The entrepreneurial rather than bureaucratic nature of the groups gives founders broad latitude in shaping their programs, allowing them to draw on "cultured capacities" learned from work, family, or religious life.[1] This chapter shows that religion operates more as a flexible set of resources than a distinctive identity for grassroots international NGOs.

We have seen that grassroots INGOs are shaped less by pressures from funders or governments than by personal relationships with individual donors, brokers, and aid recipients. But while the leaders of grassroots INGOs have relative freedom in the models they employ, they face several acute challenges compared with other aid organizations. This chapter shows religion as a case of *how* those personal relationships are converted into the resources needed for development work. One of grassroots INGOs' fundamental tasks is to gain a foothold in prospective field sites and to build effective relationships there. They lack connections with host country governments and the other institutions with which large aid agencies typically collaborate. Here grassroots INGOs use religious networks to gain introductions and to develop the brokerage relationships discussed in chapter 5. Second, grassroots INGOs' voluntary status and small size means that they lack professional legitimacy vis-à-vis potential supporters and partners. Grassroots INGO leaders can try to build legitimacy with religious discourse that frames their chosen projects in religious traditions of charitable action—or that even suggests divine sanction for the activities (the discursive move that Natalie was reluctant to make). Finally, these organizations rely almost exclusively on individual donors within the leaders' personal networks for money and labor. I show below ways that these leaders repurpose familiar religious modes of action about charitable giving—to varying levels of success.

Analyzing religion in terms of the resources it affords aid groups is consistent with the empirical realities of the contemporary aid field and with prevailing theory about the fragmented and context-dependent nature of religion.[2] Grassroots international NGOs have emerged in an era in which the lines between "religious" and "secular" approaches to international development have been blurring. In 1998, the World Bank instituted the World Faiths Development Dialogue, and subsequently the Swiss, Swedish, and British foreign aid agencies launched various initiatives related to the role of religion in development. (The US Agency for International Development was meanwhile included in the George W. Bush administration's broader effort to engage faith-based organizations with federal agencies.) At the same time, religious aid organizations came to cooperate more closely with and to resemble their secular counterparts. Nearly two-thirds of all private overseas aid was administered by church-associated organizations between 1946 and 1953.[3] But as denominational aid agencies began to accept contracts and grants from the US government beginning in the 1970s, their distinctive religious identities became compartmentalized or were abandoned altogether. A study by Kniss and Campbell of sixty-three American religious aid groups in the late 1990s showed that religious identities had little effect on organizations' program size or finances.[4] Ethnographic studies of World Vision and other Christian NGOs have shown that regulations from funders, the sensibilities of host governments, and the normative pressures of professional aid work press those NGOs to behave more like their secular counterparts.[5]

I make two theoretical assumptions about religion in this analysis. The first, relatively uncontroversial one, is that religion must be studied as a social phenomenon—existing between people and within particular contexts—and not simply a matter of the relationship between an individual and the divine. The second assumption is that humans' behavior around religion, as in other domains, is *incongruent*—that is, religious beliefs and action are fragmented and inconsistent; people invoke them differently in different contexts.[6] Religious incongruence aligns with a broader theoretical understanding of culture that does not expect people to behave in consistent ways according to deep-seated values or dispositions. Rather, people draw on ideas and practices from a cultural "tool kit," acting strategically according to their context, and producing behavior that is not always consistent with professed ideas, and ideas that are not always consistent with one another.[7] If we are to understand aid as a personal project, we must recognize the ways that aid givers and receivers manipulate multiple roles, skills, and types of language. Natalie's words at the beginning of the chapter show that dichotomies between "faith-based" and "secular" organizations are difficult, and when made by an analyst, even misleading. Instead of assuming that "religious people" or "religious organizations" will behave in certain ways, I show here how religion affords resources to grassroots INGOs that the leaders can strategically use for the organizations' benefit.

First, religion offers *networks*, or helps create the relationships themselves. Religion also provides symbolic resources that motivate and shape supporters' action. Grassroots INGOs can draw on religious *frames*, or symbols that help people understand their work in ways that have shared meaning, as well as *modes of action*, or familiar practices, that can be repurposed for the benefit of grassroots INGOs.

Networks

Religious networks play critical roles for grassroots INGOs in recruiting supporters and offering entrée to aid-receiving communities. Grassroots INGOs rely on personal networks of their founders to collect the goods and labor to initiate their projects. Colleagues, neighbors, family, and friends figure prominently in this support network—as do religious congregations, which often overlap with circles of family and friends. (Natalie and Erasto's stories illustrate this pattern.) When I refer to religious *networks*, I mean three qualities of the social structure of religion in the United States. First, religious congregations serve as pools of likely volunteers and donors. Existing research has demonstrated that congregational membership influences the likeliness, extent, and recipients of people's volunteer hours and money.[8] Recruiting support through a congregation is more efficient for grassroots INGO leaders than contacting potential donors one at a time. Second, congregations are highly embedded organizations: members of congregations are likely to be member of other sorts of associations, which makes cross-cutting flows of resources more likely.[9] Third, religion is structured by denominations and other sorts of formal organizational networks that increasingly cross national borders.[10] Individuals and congregations in these networks supply grassroots INGOs with critical cash, labor, meeting space, and in-kind goods. And while larger aid agencies can initiate their work through partnerships with foundations, receiving country governments, or UN agencies, grassroots INGOs often gain footholds in developing countries through global religious networks.

Except for other NGOs, religious congregations are the most common network partner cited by grassroots INGOs on their websites. Forty percent of grassroots INGOs have some sort of partnership with a religious congregation. Of the 64 grassroots INGOs with a congregational partner in the sample of 150 organizations, the share that have partnerships with a US congregation only, a receiving country congregation only, and with both types are roughly equal. Religious congregations are more common partners than either foreign or US governments, businesses, foundations, arts groups, schools or universities, or diaspora organizations.

Websites depict religious networks as playing a critical role in furnishing donations and volunteers. Congregations can be important stops on fundraising tours; a grassroots INGO that supports Tibetan Buddhism raised money through a series of visits by a well-known monk to US meditation centers, yoga studios, and interfaith churches. Congregations also often provide recruitment pools for teams of volunteers that travel together for a week or two at a time. Most often these groups are referred to as "mission teams," reflecting the religious frames that are shared by the grass-roots INGOs and congregations. Grassroots INGOs that named US congregations as partners on their website were more likely to solicit American volunteers to come abroad (43%) than those who list no such partnership (32%). All case study organizations except Indego Africa solicited short-term volunteers, and For Kenya's Tomorrow and Wellsprings of Hope recruited explicitly from part-ner congregations. These volunteers would often bring with them donations such as stationery items for schools, laptop computers, medical supplies, and small gifts for children. Once they arrived in country, their tasks varied. More skilled volunteers or those with longer relationships with the grassroots INGOs might run training workshops for African doctors, teachers, or nurses. Less-skilled volunteers might play with children or paint school buildings.

Scholars of both short-term missions and international volun-teering have begun to question whether short-term volunteers' contributions to aid efforts are worth the expense.[11] After all, would it not be more efficient to contribute volunteers' travel costs toward actual project expenses? Couldn't much of the labor be hired locally, especially for low-skill tasks? In my case study inter-views, American grassroots INGO leaders—and to my surprise, African leaders—said that the contributions of short-term volun-teers were worth the expense and hassle. They recognize that short-term volunteers would not realistically donate the amount they spend on travel. For these volunteers, the trips abroad replace vacations or other leisure-time activities. Natalie of FKT and sev-eral board members of Wellsprings of Hope explained that short-term trips ratchet up supporters' commitment to the organization. Trips abroad become the springboard for future financial support or membership on the board. Existing research suggests that this is a dicey proposition: ver Beek demonstrated that 162 short-term missionaries to Honduras gave on average only $2 more per person, per year after their trip than before.[12] But grassroots INGOs, operating on small budgets, do not think in terms of marginal gains among large numbers of givers; instead, they hope for major commitments from a handful, and sometimes they get them. Clara, a supporter of For Kenya's Tomorrow, came to volunteer full-time for four months in Kenya after a shorter trip. Evan, the volunteer for Activate Tanzania, was convinced by villagers to raise money to build a preschool. He returned home and raised nearly $20,000.

Several African brokers for grassroots INGOs emphasized that they enjoyed the exchange with American visitors. Paul, a Ugandan pastor who is one of the local leaders of Wellsprings of Hope, explained the utility of American volunteers in another way. "Our people, they are very, very careful and attentive to a foreigner, the volunteer, to what he is speaking; . . . they hear and they trust the words of the volunteers." He believed that American strangers are trusted more than Ugandan strangers also claiming to do good, because Ugandans have seen too many charlatans among their own countrymen. From his perspective, why would it be worth an American's time to come halfway across the world for a swindle?

It was denominational networks that offered beachheads to three of the case study NGOs. The opening section of this chapter explained how the global network of Lutheran churches that links Tanzania and Minnesota helped give rise to Activate Tanzania. Wellsprings of Hope had its beginning in a visit from a Texas delegation of Baptist pastors, and the initial goal was to provide financial support for the ministry of five Ugandan Baptist pastors. When Natalie of For Kenya's Tomorrow first traveled to that country with only a vague idea of the work she might do, a church friend sent her with an introduction to the leader of a fellow Open Bible church in Nairobi. In all three cases, denominational ties from the United States to churches and to specific pastors or dioceses in Africa provided an accessible entry point for Americans interested in aid work.

The embedded quality of religious congregations is important even for groups like the Rwanda Ultrasound Initiative that did not invoke religious language in their websites or in interviews and that did not carry out any evangelistic tasks. The two professional associations of emergency medicine physicians were the most important recruiting networks for RUI, but one of the physicians on the board had given a fundraising talk at her parents' friends' church. RUI had no qualms about using religious networks as a resource, even though its leaders spoke in interviews about the importance of separating religious practice from the provision of medical care.

Frames

Religion also offers grassroots INGOs resources that serve as "cultural blueprints" to motivate and guide supporters' action.[13] By drawing on these blueprints, NGOs activate ways of thinking and acting that have been cultivated in religious contexts of supporters' lives. Like other organizations trying to mobilize people for social change, grassroots INGOs engage in *framing*—that is, organizing, rendering meaningful, and simplifying the problems of poverty and the group's proposed solutions.[14] The projects that grassroots INGOs carry out could be (and historically have been) framed in several ways. Schooling and agriculture were framed as "civilizing" processes under colonial regimes, in the post–World War II era as part of "modernization," and most recently as "development" or "poverty alleviation."[15] Religion affords leaders of grassroots INGOs the capacity to frame these tasks as part of religious traditions of charity, altruism, or mission. Crucially, these frames legitimate action by grassroots actors—one does not need an advanced degree or government mandate to intervene in the problem of poverty.

By *frame* I mean "a lens through which we observe and interpret social life . . . [that can] highlight certain aspects of social life and hide or block others."[16] When grassroots INGOs use religious frames, they highlight religious rationales for charity and sometimes for particular projects or classes of recipients. Other religious discourse can suggest a calling or a divine sanction to a group's work. As theory suggests, most grassroots INGOs alternate between religious and secular frames (e.g., human rights, humanitarianism); exclusive use of religious frames for NGOs' work is constraining, given the multiple audiences they face.

Religious language is a common feature of NGO websites, and importantly, it can be used to frame both explicitly religious tasks (proselytizing, training pastors) and "secular" social welfare projects like providing clean water. Of 150 websites, 40 groups framed their work with rationales of enacting God's will or demonstrating God's love. (Another single group referred to Islamic virtue to rationalize its work.) Of these, less than half (18) carried out what I have described as Christian ministry tasks: proselytizing, training pastors, building churches. The rest were using religious framing to rationalize the education, small business, medical, and clean water projects that have been described elsewhere.

A prime example of religious framing comes from the group Living Water International. On a page of the site titled "Why Water?," the organization offers a number of reasons why water and sanitation are pressing issues for development. The page cites statistics on water-borne illness from the World Health Organization and the medical journal the *Lancet*: water-related diseases cause 2.2 million deaths a year, and roughly two thousand children succumb to diarrheal diseases each day in Africa. But the most prominent text on the page frames water in terms of the gospel: "For Living Water it's all about Jesus. It's about demonstrating God's love, announcing his kingdom, seeing Jesus in the least of our brothers and sisters, offering a cup of water in Jesus' name and proclaiming his gospel, the living water. Helping communities create sustainable water, sanitation, hygiene, and Christian witness programs in partnership with local churches is just the best way we've found to do that. Why? Because the water crisis affects poverty, women, health and education—and for us it's a spiritual issue." The grassroots INGO's name and this text refer to two passages in the gospel of John where Jesus speaks of living water: "If any one thirst, let him come to me and drink. He who believes in me, as the scripture has said, 'Out of his heart shall flow rivers of living water.'"[17] The group uses claims from development experts about the effect of water shortages on women, health, education, and poverty. But using the phrase "living water" invokes the ministry of Jesus and suggests to the reader that digging wells is in continuity with that ministry. The allusion allows the group to say, "for us it's a spiritual issue," and to enlist supporters on the basis of the project's religious bona fides.

Tying a project to a passage of scripture is one way to frame it as "religious." Other techniques are to describe the project as a vessel of God's love, or to claim that it arose from God's call to an individual to carry it out. Even projects without an explicit biblical link or in common traditions of religious charity can be framed as expressions of God's love, as seen by the discourse of an NGO doing women's enterprise projects: "OneMaker exists to be a tangible expression of God's love to poor women and girls vulnerable to trafficking and other exploitation by giving opportunities through education and business ventures. We provide educational sponsorships to girls in poverty, believing their God-given potential is a treasure and should be developed" (OneMaker).[19] In this text, "potential"—intellectual and economic—is a gift from God, and programs that support that potential are an extension of God's love.

It is not uncommon in these texts for grassroots INGO leaders—or volunteers for the organization, posting blogs or comments on the website—to offer narratives of God "calling" them to start the organization or to engage in a certain project. In one example, the leader of a group that operates orphan programs in Africa blogs about a late-night prayer session in which she is told to prepare a space for infants. In an account from the Friends of UNIFAT website, a Ugandan woman describes her desolation after the civil war in that country, and how a prayer "led" her to start a school that would later receive support from an American NGO: "As I prayed to be shown what to do, I was led to the parable about the sower who went sowing seeds. . . . I knew then that the good ground could represent children and the sower could be I; the seeds could be the good information, or teaching imparted to the children. I knew that the time had come. In the spring of 1983 I returned home to start a school among my people."

Describing one's efforts as led by God can do several kinds of discursive work. It might presage success, or potential for success, especially if it is linked with religious narratives with a known outcome. A reader of this text who is familiar with the parable of the seeds knows that the seeds sown on "good ground" bear fruit. If

God brought this text to the woman's mind, along with the vision of a school, a reader may believe that God will bless the school's efforts with "fruits." Second, describing one's efforts as a calling can justify the choice of a particular place or type of project that might otherwise seem arbitrary. After a civil war, why start a school, rather than rebuilding houses or sheltering orphans? Claiming one is "shown what to do" by God provides justification for a particular approach to complex problems of poverty.

Modes of Action

Having recruited supporters through religious networks, grass-roots INGO leaders can draw on religious modes of action in which these individuals are already fluent. The turn toward practice in the study of religion has emphasized the habits or patterns of action that religion affords.[18] Here, the many things that people have learned to do in religious life—cook, pray, give money—are deployed for the good of aid projects. Religious modes of action taken on behalf of grassroots INGOs fall into two broad types: first, repertoires of asking for and giving time and other support; second, repertoires of religious practice that provide shared activities for Americans and locals in aid-receiving countries.

Natalie, the founder of For Kenya's Tomorrow, told me that her short-term mission trips provided a mode of action for raising FKT's early funds. As a teenager she had sent a letter to extended family and friends asking for contributions for her travel. People were willing to contribute small amounts, she told me. They did so again when Natalie started FKT. She added that her parents had been on the receiving end of many similar letters from missionaries over the years, and that they typically made small contributions;

people understood that this is how mission work was paid for. Her childhood church also saw support for FKT as part of its missions repertoire—Natalie and her husband are pictured, wearing matching FKT T-shirts, in the church's directory of missionaries.

Another religious practice of giving harnessed by grassroots INGOs is the Muslim obligation of *zakat*, used by two groups in the website sample. These groups carried out education and sanitation projects, but also distributed food aid during Ramadan. One of these groups, based in Dayton, Ohio, and called HOPE, further allows donors to designate their contributions as *zakat al-maal*, alms given as a "tax" of one's wealth to the poor, or *zakat al-fitr*, alms given on the holiday of *Eid-al-fitr*.

Prayer is another religious mode of action exploited by grassroots INGOs. The websites of 19 of 150 NGOs explicitly asked the reader to pray for the success of the organization. In these texts, prayer is often presented as a way for those who are unable to volunteer overseas to support the organization; in some cases, readers are encouraged to pray about how they can best contribute to the organization, making prayer a stepping stone to further commitment. Circle of Hope, which has a variety of projects in a community in Malawi, wrote that it was starting a "24 hour prayer team . . . for the ministry and vision that Jesus has given us for the healing of Africa." The post continued with a guide for prayer adapted from a book by evangelist missionary E. Stanley Jones. But just as grassroots INGOs draw on both religious and nonreligious frames, they concurrently use religious and nonreligious modes of action. The blog post on Circle of Hope's website immediately following the prayer team announcement was about an animal husbandry project—readers were asked to donate money to buy chickens and goats.

Grassroots INGOs operate in a broader context in which media and migration diffuse religious practices across borders.[19] "Bridging" modes of action helps grassroots INGOs reinforce religious networks, building trust and providing a starting point for on-the-ground collaboration between Americans and local partners. Informants from two case study NGOs told me that "prayer walks" were one of the activities that American volunteers shared with the NGOs' local leadership. A small group of Americans and locals would set out on foot in a neighborhood, calling on each house and asking if they could pray with them. Wellsprings of Hope operates in a Ugandan town that has a slight Muslim majority, and one informant told me that they made calls to both Muslim and Christian households: "We just pray together, Muslim, Christian, it doesn't really matter. . . . Very few people don't want to be prayed for." Clara, a twenty-two-year-old American woman who volunteers with For Kenya's Tomorrow, told me that prayer walks and Bible studies were the main tasks on which she was able to collaborate with young Kenyan men. The young men knew the neighborhood and provided local knowledge and safety to the volunteers; the walks helped the volunteers meet neighbors and understand local conditions, which would help them carry out future work.

Among the case study groups, worship services were also part of the repertoire shared by Americans and African Christians. The American and Kenyan Pentecostals I met through FKT were familiar with the same songs and preachers through the global broadcasts of the Australian Pentecostal church Hillsong. Volunteers from Wellsprings of Hope and Activate Tanzania also mentioned joining African counterparts in worship. Several of these volunteers recounted the "liveliness" of these worship services, which they felt was different from their American style of worship, but they said that despite the differences, the shared worship had afforded solidarity. Their narratives were consistent with Wuthnow's claim in his study of globalized Christianity that common worship "increase[s] the sense among widely scattered congregations that they share a common destiny and bear responsibility for one another."[20] This sense of shared destiny may be more imagined than factual, but it is likely to be emotionally salient for American supporters. Shared religious practice becomes a means by which personal relationships are nurtured between Americans and people in aid-receiving communities.

Yet grassroots INGO volunteers saw some religious modes of action as potentially damaging to their organization's goals. Two of the RUI physicians described themselves as personally religious, but they drew a firm line between their own beliefs and any expression of religion in the delivery of medical care. (One of these physicians invited me and my research assistant to light Shabbat candles with him at the end of a long day of volunteering.) The founder of RUI disparaged the display of religion during medical care as "a bartering system"—medical attention in exchange for being proselytized. RUI volunteers rejected the language of mission. Said one: "Of course, there's very good things that missionaries have done. But we're not in that day and age anymore, so I think you have to be a little bit careful."

This volunteer's comment about bartering points to one of the perils of bridging religious modes of action: by emphasizing sameness, they can mask inequalities in power between Americans and aid recipients. The RUI volunteers were explicit about the power inequity between people giving and receiving medical care, and were wary that religious expression that tried to "bridge" that gap could in fact be coercive. Here is an instance where RUI volunteers' practice as secular medical professionals prevailed over religious action.

· · ·

Americans are a highly religious people compared with citizens of other industrialized countries; surveys show that the share of Americans who say religion is important in their life more closely resembles patterns in Africa and Latin American than in Europe.[21] This religiosity provides tools for grassroots INGOs to connect with people of faith in the Global South, and it offers cultural blueprints for mobilizing American supporters.

Rather than looking at *whether* grassroots INGOs are religious, I have argued, we should look at *how* religion operates within them. The interviews and analyses of websites presented here have shown that people involved with aid work classify organizations as "religious" in different ways than researchers might, and that religious networks, frames, and modes of action are only part of the broader tool kits deployed by these people. While this chapter has focused on what religion affords, I have pointed to instances where religious resources are inadequate or are set aside in favor of other resources.

Like larger aid agencies, grassroots INGOs need income, public legitimacy, and local partners. But they meet these needs without the advantages of name recognition, professional training and staff, or connections with host country governments or UN agencies. Chapter 5 showed that personal relationships are critical to motivating people to be involved in grassroots INGOs, and the trust embedded in those relationships is crucial for the groups' function. By looking at religion, we can see how those relationships are established in the first place. We can also see the important cultural glue that binds those relationships together, through shared symbolism of religious narratives and images, and the shared meaningful action that occurs in religious practice.

Conclusion

Possibilities and Perils of Amateur Aid

One of the unanticipated benefits of my fieldwork in Africa was the opportunity to walk in the shoes of grassroots INGOs' volunteers. Like them, I got the pre-trip vaccinations and malaria drugs, took the long and uncomfortable flight, and arrived in a country where my skin color made me a conspicuous visitor. As an American visitor to these NGOs, I was courted as a prospective donor. I received the grand tour of projects, was introduced around, dined, and briefed on the needs of the organization. And by the end of my visit, I got the pitch: that when I returned home I would "remember" them and "advocate" for them. That I would pray for their success as they would pray for mine. In one instance, I gave an envelope with a modest cash donation; I saw that my financial resources and networks had far greater purchasing power in East Africa than they do in the United States.

More recently, those networks came into play when I learned about a full scholarship opportunity for African students. A family member was in a position to "advocate" for good candidates, and I was asked if I knew of any. I did: the first teacher hired at the school run by Activate Tanzania. He was born in the village and returned to teach at the new secondary school, having been one of only a handful of young people in a generation to achieve post-primary education. He started tutoring village students for the school before he was ever paid a penny and had stayed on at the school despite high staff turnover. He had told me he deeply hoped to continue a university education. His story was perfect! He could win one of these scholarships! I would change his life!

Those were the key words: I would change his life. I would be like a fairy godmother. My connections to an American university, commonplace here, would be like magic in an African context. This is what I had heard, in other words, in so many interviews. Because American resources go so much further in developing countries, they can be transformative. There is an allure that Americans can come in, and with a phone call here and a few thousand dollars there, change someone's life. In fact, the idea of "changing lives" is more of what I heard from grassroots INGOs than "changing the world." Changing the world is a political act. Changing a life is a personal one.

This episode showed me the allure of personal aid that defines and animates grassroots INGOs. These groups are a reinvented form of the NGOs that have been rising actors in international affairs generally and in development specifically since World War II. The Anglo tradition of using charitable organizations to address social problems met with particular political opportunities: the push to develop Third World countries during the Cold War, and later rising neoliberalism that outsourced state functions to private actors. As NGOs began carrying out major projects on behalf of bilateral and multilateral donors, they professionalized. Like nonprofit organizations in other domains that shifted "from membership to management," US-based development NGOs became organizations run by credentialed experts.[1] The organizations were shaped by the dynamics of a field of professionalized organizations that included NGOs, for-profit contractors, and government and intergovernmental donor agencies. Resource constraints and logistical pressures also worked against amateur aid efforts in the mid-twentieth century. Aid agencies funded from abroad had to rely on the limited networks of paved roads and phone lines, which usually meant expensive office compounds in capital cities and regional towns. American citizens interested in supporting development either had to dedicate their career to it (or at least two years, if they could be chosen as Peace Corps volunteers) or confine themselves to charitable donations.

But as the twentieth century ended, it became dramatically easier to move people, money, goods, and messages to remote corners of the world. Globalization transformed a number of domains for charitable and political action. Cheap travel and more importantly, the ability to communicate from Brooklyn to Butare by email and text message, have drastically reduced reliance on older forms of organization. For development aid, as for protest movements and ethical consumerism, globalization has enabled new organizational forms that emphasize individual action.

This book has attempted, like the blind men "seeing" the elephant, a morphology of this new organizational form. The case studies here helped us answer the question, *How do these organizations start?* We saw that the globalized movement of people paved the way for grassroots INGOs. Two of the founders, one an expatriate and one who would become a naturalized citizen, spent their youth in Africa; another made her way there through a study exchange, while others took part in religious mission trips. When these Americans reached moments in their lives when they wanted to "do something more," they reached out to friends, family, colleagues, and fellow congregants. The groups now run projects that range from direct service provision to micro-enterprise training on budgets of tens to hundreds of thousands of dollars. On certain dimensions there is tremendous diversity among the Americans involved in these groups. As the case study organizations showed, some of the founders hold terminal degrees and have spent their lives traveling, while others have built their lives around family and church. Some use the language of God's love and calling to explain their work, while others believe that religion has no place in the delivery of aid; some are retirees while others work fifty-plus hours a week. They are Democrats and Republicans. Some are "professionals" of some stripe—attorneys, doctors, clergy—but none were experienced aid workers. All were motivated less by a critique of existing development approaches than by an impulse to get their own hands dirty and the belief that they had skills worth sharing. All struggled to develop programs that made sense in aid-receiving communities, and all came to rely on local brokers to help them make halting progress.

How do grassroots INGOs understand development? It is easier than ever before for everyday Americans like these to forge ties to developing countries, but the goals of development itself have become broader and more elusive. While amateur aid workers might be able to help build bring about the "plentiful crops" and "houses with tight roofs" that were the aims of the late 1950s, they are ill-equipped to deal with the trade imbalances, civil conflict, environmental degradation, and malfunctioning political institutions that were defined as development problems by the turn of the millennium. But these issues seem beside the point to many Americans who encounter poverty firsthand and feel compelled to personally act. Patients are suffering when medical technology is not used: "I found these machines . . . but if they don't know how to use it, then it's totally wasted, and it's this amazing technology." Young children are denied education: "We were seeing three-year-old kids not being able to go to school, but they have to walk miles back and forth while they're carrying big water jugs." In response, Americans start their own organizations that afford them opportunities that are impossible in other aid settings: working directly with beneficiaries on projects of their own design, drawing on skills developed in work and civic life.

The leaders of grassroots INGOs can be part-time volunteers whose primary commitments are still to their own career and personal networks. They are not socialized in the graduate degree programs or career circuits of full-time aid workers. Instead, grassroots INGOs are based in communities in every state of the union and operate with few ties to the professionalized aid field. Not constrained by resource dependence on donor agencies or the normative pressures of the professionalized field, grassroots INGOs' discourse and practices take shape consistent with the religious memberships, civic experiences, and personal lives of their leaders. Americans' family histories of socioeconomic mobility and personal vocational skills often define the organizations' aid projects.

Like larger aid agencies, grassroots INGOs need income, public legitimacy, and local partners. But they meet these needs without the advantages of name recognition, professional training and staff, or connections with host country governments or UN agencies. Grassroots INGOs turn to personal relationships to supply these resources. The organizations look to family and friends in the United States to provide cash and labor, while they look to brokers in the South to execute projects, provide local feedback, and offer emotionally satisfying partnerships. Personal relationships, as we have seen, provide the motivation and partners for Americans to launch new organizations.

For many grassroots INGOs, religious networks help establish those relationships. Religion can also provide important cultural glue that binds those relationships together, through shared symbolism of religious narratives and images, and the shared meaningful action that occurs in religious practice. Religion, in other words, affords a set of valuable resources that allow decentralized forms of aid to flourish. My depiction of the way religion operates in grassroots INGOs also challenges depictions of NGOs as highly rationalized and secular, or at least highly compartmentalized. Recall that even as FKT's Natalie met with engineering experts on biogas toilets, she referred to "my conversations with God" as the major influence on strategic decisions for the organization. Texans and Ugandans both told me that God had worked through nine-year-old Lindsey to provide funds for Wellsprings of Hope and that shared faith is at the heart of their partnership.

What do grassroots INGOs do, where do they go, and whom do they serve? Grassroots INGOs' aid diverges from the official development assistance distributed by the US government in its destination and sectors. ODA is driven not just by perceived "need" but by national interest, and projects to which it is devoted are shaped by a combination of political objectives and expert judgment.[2] Grassroots INGOs, however, go to places where Americans have built networks through migration, tourism, work, and study. More than half of grassroots INGOs have at least one project in Africa, with roughly a third working in Asia and a quarter in Latin America. The groups are especially prone to working in Anglophone countries, and existing tourist infrastructure makes it easy for novice volunteers to get their footing. Women and children are the most common beneficiaries of grassroots INGO projects, which tend toward education, small business training, and provision of clean water and medical care. These projects are often implemented in partnership with other NGOs or congregations. Websites suggest that work with receiving-country governments is rare, and the case studies indicated that although some grassroots INGOs aim for meaningful local partnership, the more common approach is to make only the gestures needed to keep local authorities out of one's hair.

The work carried out by grassroots INGOs can be distilled into three models. The least common, the social relations model, works through cultural exchange, advocacy, and capacity building: it aims to help beneficiaries in the Global South build collective skills or relationships that will improve standards of living in the long run. More often, grassroots INGOs direct their aid at individuals rather than collectivities. About a third of grassroots INGOs aim to transform people's skills and dispositions, with the theory that more educated or business-minded individuals will be able to lift themselves—and eventually the people around them—out of poverty. But more than half operate the sort of programs that mainstream development INGOs abandoned (at least officially) decades ago—directly providing goods and services to aid recipients.

I have argued that a strong role for the individual is a defining characteristic of new globalized approaches to activism and aid. For grassroots INGOs, this manifests in the way that they depict heroic individuals as the agents of development. Aid recipients are either portrayed as suffering or as heroic; descriptions of them refer to their qualities of hard work, kindness, and ambition. Stories of personal transformation abound. A majority of grassroots INGO projects operate on the assumption that if individuals are provided with the right stuff or the right skills, their lives will be transformed. These transformed people will then go on to lift up the people around them. One of my arguments in this book is that whether they resemble more closely Korten's first- or his second-generation models, what grassroots INGO approaches have in common is the idea of *development as a personal process.* This vision emphasizes the power of the individual and contagion effects to create social change. Grassroots INGOs might successfully transfer skills (e.g., knowledge of water-borne illness), but they rarely help cultivate the local institutions (a government capable of maintaining public sanitation) needed to sustainably apply them.

I have shown that globalization provides spaces to resist the pressures of professionalization—but tenuously. The independence of grassroots INGOs hinges on their small budgets and ability to self-finance. Leaders of Indego Africa and Wellsprings of Hope, the case study groups with the largest budgets, expressed concern that increased logistical demands of expanded programs worked against the personal ethos that was at the heart of their organizations. As long as grassroots INGOs rely on personal networks of individual donors to finance their work, there are few pressures to quantify their outputs. Yet all five case study organizations said that expanding their work would require winning grants, and foundation gifts almost inevitably come with demands for greater formalization.[3] This pressure hints at two possible paths for the grassroots INGOs that persist. One is to maintain low-budget, self-financed projects and remain structured something like minimalist organizations.[4] The other is to expand with government and foundation funding and to have a structure that aligns with those funders' requirements, eventually functioning as a traditional aid NGO.

Those have mainly been the fates of the case study organizations in the decade and a half since their origins.[5] The activities of For Kenya's Tomorrow have largely been handed over to other organizations as the founder has settled full-time in the United States with her Kenyan husband and two small children. Three groups have persisted on small budgets and have maintained their voluntary ethos, while Indego Africa has grown into a small but quasi-professionalized NGO. It employs American interns with work and educational backgrounds in development and business and a handful of paid staff in its New York office.

How Should We Assess Grassroots INGOs?

We live in a world where a four-hour flight can transport Americans to places with standards of living that the United States overcame a century or more ago. Policies related to trade or intellectual property seem coldly esoteric to the American that encounters makeshift huts and latrines on a volunteer trip to Haiti. The narrative of development as a personal process wielded by grassroots INGOs is an attempt to make sense of American volunteers' relative affluence, and to account for it in terms that offer the same hopeful possibilities for people living in developing countries. Grassroots INGO aid is an improvised, imperfect, personal, human response to the poverty Americans can now witness thanks to globalization.

Grassroots international NGOs are best understood as supply-driven organizations with strong expressive characteristics. They emerge from the entrepreneurial initiative of a founder whose own tastes and energies play a determining role in shaping the organization. The origin stories of the case study organizations in this book all portray individuals with tremendous energy who found the support of family and friends to put their charitable impulses into action. As these groups took shape, most came to provide some kind of service or training to beneficiaries—they developed instrumental goals—but we would misunderstand these groups if we thought that efficient transmission of these goods was the priority. The efficiency and rigor prized by professionalized organizations takes a secondary place for grassroots INGOs.

These groups prize probity—they know the money is not being siphoned off to buy imported Audis—but there is little pressure for quantifiable results. Grassroots INGOs are spared the inefficiencies of trying to measure and monitor changes that are subtle and slow. They can choose projects that work simply in one place, rather than chasing silver bullets that will guarantee future funding. The groups "look" efficient because they rarely pay for office space or salaries (though a real accounting of time and goods donated would paint a different picture). But in certain dimensions, grassroots INGOs are highly inefficient. They often use American labor when local workers would be cheaper and more knowledgeable. They solicit in-kind donations and haul these goods overseas when they could buy them more cheaply where they are working, and stimulate the local economy to boot. And they rarely have learned from past successes and failures in development, even in the countries or communities where they work. Pastor Bill Smith could live with the inefficiency of "reinventing the wheel" because "it was OUR wheel." The ability to express values of tolerance, solidarity, and generosity are at the heart of people's attraction to grassroots INGOs, as shown in interviews with Natalie ("I wanted it to be an open door for people to come and serve") and Leann (who wanted to reach her intolerant, "uneducated family members").

One difficulty with allowing expressive rationales to drive voluntary action is that there is a fine line between enacting one's values through action and simply "feeling good." The nonprofit organizations we have most often thought of as "expressive" in developed countries are advocacy, arts, and recreational groups—that is, civic groups where people are acting for their own collective benefit rather than for a client. But there are complications when people use organizations that provide services to disadvantaged people to also serve their expressive purposes. Nina Eliasoph observed this in an American after-school tutoring program for disadvantaged youth that was staffed largely by college-student and middle-aged volunteers. Eager to become like "beloved aunties" and have emotionally satisfying encounters with these youth, the volunteers sometimes undermined the program's educational goals by distracting students from their work or choosing to work with the friendlier teenagers. Eliasoph argued, further, that the intimacy that volunteers craved in these short encounters was not a realistic goal; the meaningful relationships that flowered were between the youth and the program director, who was there every day, week after week. The closeness of those relationships did not always feel good; discord between the director and the youth was a regular occurrence. Yet "it was the kind of intimacy that means familiarity and comfort with a unique person, place, or activity, which slowly accretes over time—very different from the quick intensity that the plug-in volunteers sought."[6] Grassroots INGOs face similar risks from their volunteers' desire for emotional satisfaction. The intensity of volunteering for a grassroots INGO is heightened by the foreignness of the context and the sense that the needs one confronts are real and unmet. When expressive goals are pursued through emotionally satisfying relationships with beneficiaries, instrumental and expressive goals are likely to be at odds.

The near-collapse of Wellsprings of Hope showed the peril of this arrangement. Bound by friendship and shared religious beliefs, the American leaders of the group imposed almost no formal measures of financial accountability on the local brokers until it was apparent that one of the brokers had embezzled thousands of dollars. The founder of the organization had been reluctant to believe that one of his "best friends" could do such a thing. But even when there is no malfeasance, these brokers occupy untenable positions of having to represent the interests of themselves, local citizens, and the American leaders. Grassroots INGOs are likely to find that they need to sacrifice the emotional satisfaction of personal relationships to develop forms of downward accountability that tie in to local social structures.

The supply-driven or personal dimension of grassroots INGO aid has promises and perils. One of the conventional arguments in favor of supply-driven organizations is their capacity for innovation; the nonprofit form provides a place for people to experiment with new approaches to solving social problems. While most grassroots INGOs carry out highly conventional—and even outdated—projects, Indego Africa and the Rwanda Ultrasound Initiative showed that these groups can innovate. Indego took a micro-enterprise model and paired it with fair-trade pricing and rigorous training in partnership with a local NGO. RUI took point-of-care ultrasound, a technique favored in US emergency medicine, and is teaching (and learning) how this can be deployed in African hospitals with limited resources. It is not yet clear whether these innovations will be successful enough to be adopted by other nonprofit, government, or for-profit actors.

One of the perils of supply-driven approaches is that the programs envisioned by the founders are poor fits in the local context. This is hardly a new problem in the aid world. James Ferguson famously described a Canadian aid agency's failed attempt to improve agricultural production in Lesotho, which overlooked the fact that the region's residents were not farmers but migrant laborers in South African mines.[7] But if all aid organizations risk oversimplifying or misdiagnosing development problems, grassroots INGOs are vulnerable to doing so in particular ways (that require particular remedies). First, the leaders of grassroots INGOs typically have less knowledge of the local context than mainstream INGOs. Leaders—even emigrants like Erasto—spend only weeks or months of the year in the field and instead rely on the reports of their local brokers. Many grassroots INGO leaders have few local language skills and must rely on translators or ask locals to speak English. Important information can be lost in translation or go unheard as Americans are deaf to the small conversations taking place around them. American leaders lack not only codified knowledge of the professional development field, they also lack the contextual knowledge of the past development efforts—failed or successful—at their sites of operation.

Sometimes "reinventing the wheel" works. We should not negate the possibility that the old-fashioned goods or services offered by some grassroots INGOs are quite welcome. The structure of grassroots INGOs insulates them from the lessons learned by development experts, but also their notorious fads. If the organization simply wants to provide scholarships, it does not have to sell its projects to donors as post-conflict reconstruction or HIV prevention, for example. Ethnographic work shows that beneficiaries of aid projects often contort themselves into the projects' demands in search of cash and basic goods like bicycles, stationery, and food. When grassroots INGOs offer such goods without pretense, at least they may be satisfying their beneficiaries' wishes. If we are to critique these projects, it is basically an opportunity-cost criticism: they are handouts, and not real "development" that might change conditions instead of perpetuating a cycle of aid.

Less benignly, grassroots INGOs can be the "mere amateurs" who provide services that are of poor quality or that disappear when the providers run out of funds or interest. Given the strong role of grassroots INGOs in providing water, medical care, and education, the quality and reliability of the organizations' instrumental outputs, and not just expressive experiences, matters. I argue that this is especially important given the large share of work that targets children and the fact that most grassroots INGOs operate in countries with weak state oversight of NGOs. The issue of grassroots INGO work in orphanages is especially fraught. UNICEF has called for limiting, and in some cases, ending the practice of raising children in institutionalized care, and has called to eliminate short-term volunteer work in orphanages.[8] Many grassroots INGOs persist in both practices. A detailed analysis of whether orphanages are suitable in the places where these organizations work is not the point here; what is relevant is to say that grassroots INGOs are neither regulated in the way that such providers would be in developed countries, nor are they connected to organizations that can offer them expert advice on how best to care for orphaned children.

I have suggested that the supply-side and expressive characteristics of grassroots NGOs are what draw Americans to work through them and that these drives need tempering if these groups are to do more good than harm. Whatever their backgrounds as cowboys, grassroots INGOs cannot treat aid-receiving countries like the Wild West. They should reckon honestly with the receiving-country ministries that attempt to regulate their NGO work rather than using their small size to fly under the radar. Organizations that provide services in lieu of families or states have an obligation to meet basic standards of care, and to hold themselves accountable even if no government or professional entity is doing so. Grassroots INGOs could meet this burden by turning to support organizations like Interaction or the Accord Network, which has made efforts to include small NGOs.

Many critics of aid point out that mainstream aid agencies have become experts at "performing" local participation in development projects but not actually enacting it.[9] Grassroots INGOs that are committed to doing work that strengthens, rather than weakens, local capacity and governance can take the time to build relationships with local collectivities or help create new ones, as Indego Africa, RUI, and Activate Tanzania have done. Other forms of transnational partnerships show promise for Americans who want to contribute to development in decentralized ways but avoid the perils I have described. Community foundations are growing in Asia and Africa and are trying to create locally durable intermediaries to connect philanthropy to local grant-seeking organizations. These foundations are increasingly willing to connect small-scale foreign donors to well-vetted, locally run organizations. Such "arranged marriages" may seem less romantic to donors, but they are likely to produce more sustainable development outcomes.

Neither should compassionate Americans forget that the decisions made by Congress and their own state legislatures—even their city councils—have implications for people in the Global South. Policies about public transit, auto emission standards, and energy sources affect climate change and the billions of people who take their living from the land and sea. Refugee and immigration policies will affect those who seek to continue their educations in the United States, or those who flee the oppressive governments that NGOs work around. And when Congress debates subsidies for peanuts and cotton under the Farm Bill, the effects will ripple out to farmers clinging to their livelihoods at the edge of the Sahel.

One of the texts that recurred many times on websites to rationalize the work of grassroots INGOs was a story of a girl walking on a beach where thousands of starfish had washed up and would presumably die out of the water. The girl was picking up starfish and throwing them back in the water when a man approached her. Let it go, he told her; she could not possibly make a difference when there were so many. The girl tossed another starfish into the water and said, "I made a difference to that one."

On one hand, this allegory makes a convincing case for particularistic but limited charity. It is churlish not to recognize that many of the goods provided by grassroots INGOs—more schools, more medical care, more clean water—are of themselves good things. But the poor are not starfish, and global inequality is not the sea. Human beings have access, however complicated and politically difficult, to the forces that raise the fortunes of some nations while drowning the fortunes of others. However useful they might be to individual starfish, the Americans that support grassroots INGOs should not forget about the tides.

APPENDIX 1
Note on Methods

On Terminology

I classify grassroots international NGOs (elsewhere, "GINGOs"[1]) as a subset of international NGOs—nongovernmental organizations working in more than one country. Some writers use the term "international NGO" strictly for organizations that have distinct branches in more than one country. (Think of Oxfam, which has Oxfam GB, Oxfam USA, Oxfam India, and so on.) The Union of International Organizations' *Yearbook of International Organizations*, a data source for many sociologists studying INGOs, only includes organizations operating in three or more countries.[2] Some of the organizations described in this book would meet this definition, while many would not. All of the groups I study here are properly characterized as *transnational*—operating across national borders, albeit not necessarily using structures recognized by the state. Ultimately, in naming these groups I am less concerned about their technical organizational form than in connecting the motivations and legitimacy of Americans setting out to do aid work with their most important predecessors: mainstream international NGOs. I also distinguish grassroots international NGOs from *grassroots organizations* or GROs, which are typically understood as organizations run by the people who aim to benefit. The "grassroots" in grassroots INGOs are everyday American citizens. I intend the term *grassroots international NGOs* to productively capture the paradox between being citizen driven and international in scope, though I expect that some readers will find the language troublesome.

IRS Data

In a researcher's ideal world, every NGO would be registered with some international entity and would provide it with information on the location and aims of its projects. No such international entity exists, and NGO directories maintained by developing country governments are notoriously incomplete, contradictory, and outdated.[3]

For organizations based in the United States, IRS records provide an excellent alternative. The IRS Business Master File (BMF) contains descriptive information for all active organizations that have registered for tax-exempt status with the IRS and is updated several times a year. Two BMF files are available: one for all 501(c)3 public charities and private foundations, and another for all other tax-exempt organizations under other 501(c) subsections, such as trade unions and chambers of commerce. All of the NGOs in this study fall under the 501(c)3 designation.

An American organization that wishes to operate with tax-exempt status is generally required to apply to the IRS if it has more than $5,000 in annual revenue. The major exception is religious congregations or their full subsidiaries.[4] Until 2008, only private foundations and nonprofits with annual gross receipts of $25,000 or more were required to annually file Form 990. Since then, organizations than collect less than $25,000 (again, with the exception of religious congregations) are required to file an eight-question Form 990-N online, known as an "e-Postcard." (Beginning with tax year 2011, the ceiling for filing the e-Postcard increased to $50,000.) Organizations that fail to file for three years can be stripped of their tax-exempt status. The BMF file includes data on the location and finances of each organization, along with its unique Employer Identification Number (EIN). The BMF also lists the month and year that an organization registered with the IRS, as well as the most recent dollar amount of gross receipts from Form 990 filings.

When an organization applies for tax-exempt status with the IRS, it is given a code from the National Taxonomy of Exempt Entities according to the charitable purpose it declares on its application. NTEE codes were created in the 1980s and laboriously revised in the 2000s to increase efficiency and to better align with the North American Industry Classification System (NAICS) that was implemented by the federal government in 1999.[5] (I use the codes assigned by the National Center for Charitable Statistics, although the popular online resource Guidestar does its own NTEE coding.) Based on each code's detailed description in the NTEE-CC handbook and analysis of a sample of organizations with the relevant codes, I confine my discussion in this book to organizations with the codes Q30–Q39: International Development and Relief, and Q70 and Q71: International Human Rights. The work described in this book seems to substantively focus more on development and relief. However, as I first began to study these organizations, web searches of a random sample of organizations with these codes revealed that organizations labeled as "human rights" organizations and those labeled as "development" were carrying out very similar work. For example, a group doing women's microenterprise might be coded as Q30 or Q70 depending on whether the mission statement highlighted women's empowerment. These codes exclude international organizations without an aid mandate: international cultural exchange or study programs, groups interested in security or nonproliferation, and international trade groups. It also excludes groups that "simply send and support religious missionaries, distribute religious materials, or proselytize" without providing "some type of physical, non-religious aid."[6]

The shortcoming of this system is that organizations doing relief and development work are occasionally categorized according to the sector of their project. For instance, an organization called Development in Gardening, which does urban agriculture projects in Africa and Latin America, has code C42 (Garden Clubs). This false-negative error will conservatively bias my total count of grassroots INGOs. My analysis of the BMF found that false-positive errors—nondevelopment organizations mistakenly categorized as development organizations—were rare, about 2 percent.

NGO Websites

The second source of data for this book is grassroots INGOs' own websites. The BMF does not register organizations' websites and there is no other central clearinghouse for these addresses, so I created a database of NGO websites with help from Amazon Mechanical Turk (MTurk) workers.[7] MTurkers searched for websites that matched an organization's name and address in the BMF. To ensure the quality of the results, each organization was assigned to three MTurkers, with a research assistant resolving any conflicting findings. Of

10,684 active organizations registered with the IRS by the end of 2011, web addresses were found for 6,749. I manually removed 286 nonfunctioning sites (for example, those that yielded 404 errors, that had been taken over by bots, or posted an "Under Construction" message with no other text). I captured the text from each site using a web crawler, which yielded a corpus of thousands of text-only documents. I carried out LDA topic modeling on all 6,463 websites.[8] This allowed me to discern the major themes of those texts, and those results are published elsewhere.[9]

Drawing a random sample of grassroots INGO websites required me to determine ex ante whether the organization was "grassroots" or not. For the purposes of the website analysis presented here, I designate an NGO as "grassroots" if it was founded in 1990 or after, and if in the most recent tax year it reported $250,000 or less in revenue. The year 1990 roughly corresponds with the end of the Cold War and the beginning of the most recent era of globalization, and marks the beginning of the uptick in the number of US-registered NGOs.[10] By analyzing the 990 forms and websites of organizations at a number of revenue cutoff points, I determined that $250,000 was approximately the breaking point between organizations that employed full-time staff in the United States and those that did not, qualitatively changing them from a staffed organization to a volunteer-based one.

Of the 6,463 working websites, 72 percent were defined as grassroots INGOs by these criteria, and I drew the sample of 150 grassroots INGO websites randomly from this set. (Of active organizations in the BMF, 78 percent qualified as grassroots.) For the sample of 150 sites, I created PDF versions of the websites for analysis, including each internal page of the website but not following links to external domains. PDF files preserve most of the formatting of the original page and so are easier to read, and they provide the additional context of photographs and other graphics that are stripped away when a website is reduced to text.

I used Atlas.ti to qualitatively code each website. The simple coding tasks were to determine where each NGO is working, what sort of projects it does, and what roles volunteers and other supporters play. The more complex tasks were to code the discourse used by the NGOs about their recipients, their work, and the interaction between Americans and the purported beneficiaries. Each website was analyzed with the inductively generated codes listed in appendix 2. The codes fall into eight major categories.

- *Aid context* codes highlight text where the NGOs describe the place in which they work. These codes emphasize the ways the websites depict the geographic, economic, and political landscape of the communities being aided.
- *Role for supporters* codes flag the ways that the text referenced existing or prospective supporters of the organization—particularly the sorts of donations that are solicited, such as money or volunteer work abroad.
- *Project sector* refers to the projects the NGOs undertake. In addition to the sectors of the projects (e.g., clean water), I coded for characterizations of the projects (efficient, sustainable, etc.).
- *Partner organization* codes refer to the other organizations, such as congregations or government agencies, with which the NGO interacts in some way.
- *Photo* codes characterize the dominant image on the organization's homepage. Who or what gets most prominent billing, and how are the people depicted?
- *Rationale* codes highlight text where the NGO explains why it is doing what it is doing.
- *Recipient* codes refer to status designations of the recipients of aid (e.g., women, orphans) or qualities of those people (hardworking, living in deprived conditions) as they are depicted in the text.
- *Volunteer/staff* codes are applied to text that describes the people who run the organization. (They are typically, though not always, unpaid). This text usually comes from sections of the website entitled "About Us," "Our Board," and so on.

In chapter 4 I elaborate three models of aid based on these qualitative codes. I developed these models with a two-stage inductive method. My qualitative coding had assigned each organization to a primary project sector such as clean water, education, small business, and so on. (A complete list of these sectors appears in appendix 2). I first tallied the frequencies of codes for Rationales, Recipients, and Roles for US Supporters by primary project sector. Based on the relative frequencies of organizations within the project sectors to those categories, and using judgment based on a holistic reading of groups within those sectors, I clustered the organizations into three models of aid: Goods and Services, Skills and Dispositions, and Social Relations. Appendix 2 lists all of the grassroots INGOs in this sample and the model of aid to which I assigned them.

The website data elaborate what organizations do, where they do it, and how they frame their action for public audiences. But websites often say little about the organizational history (especially false starts and failures along the way), about the different perspectives of the group's members, or about how nascent groups learn or make decisions. To answer these questions, I turned to in-depth studies of five grassroots INGOs.

Case Studies

This book further draws on interviews, observational field notes, and documentary evidence from five organizations that I selected as case studies. For each of these organizations I carried out six to thirteen in-depth interviews with the founders, board members, key staff or volunteers, and a small number of the organization's beneficiaries. I was able to meet most of the interview subjects face to face, either in the US city where the organization is based or else in the foreign community where the organization was working. The remaining two of the forty-three interviews were carried out over Skype. My questions for supporters or employees of grassroots INGOs covered the individual's history of volunteering and civic engagement and how he or she came to be involved with or start the organization; the history of the grassroots INGO; the organization's projects and partnerships; the individual's views on poverty, development, and roles for governments, international agencies, and other actors; the role of religion in the organization; the person's experiences with the organization and the effect it has had on his or her life; and the individual's hopes or expectations for the organization's future. Interviews with beneficiaries of the project (e.g., women involved in microenterprise projects or school students) were less structured, and were aimed at capturing the participants' experiences with and opinions toward the grassroots INGO, especially as compared with other organizations in the community. The typical interview lasted ninety minutes and was digitally recorded and transcribed.

In choosing the organizations I would study in depth I looked for variations on several characteristics: the project sector in which the organizations work, the target recipients, and the size of the organization in terms of revenue and staff. I also looked to include some organizations that formally identified as religious and others that did not. (As chapter 7 shows, the question of these organizations' religiosity turned out to be more complex and interesting than I anticipated.) Finally, I looked for organizations that emerged out of different kinds of ties to developing countries. In my preliminary analysis of grassroots INGOs I observed that organizations were typically started by one of four types of people: (1) a person who had done previous volunteer work abroad and in time decided to "do more" by starting an NGO; (2) a "wonk," who in many ways resembles the volunteer but who brings some vocational expertise that is at the heart of the organization or project (often businesspeople, medical professionals, engineers, etc.); (3) a "missionary," who blends development projects with the explicitly religious aims of proselytizing, training clergy, or church planting; (4) an "immigrant-made-good," or person born abroad who comes to the United States for work or study and then sets up an organization to aid their home community.

As the research progressed, I learned that these categories were more fluid than I had anticipated and that they did not represent the most important distinctions in the way that aid was carried out. However, at the beginning of my research I sought variation on these founding types, and had one organization each from the "missionary" and "immigrant" types (Wellsprings of Hope and Activate Tanzania, respectively), two from the "wonk" type (Indego Africa and the Rwanda Ultrasound Initiative), and one from the "recommitted volunteer" type (For Kenya's Tomorrow).

As table 1 shows, two of these grassroots INGOs had revenue below the IRS reported median for international relief, development, and human rights organizations of $25,000 or less in 2011.[11] Activate Tanzania is below the 75th percentile income of $134,000, while Wellsprings of Hope is just above it. Indego Africa has the highest revenue of the case study organizations and has begun to assume some of the financial and organizational qualities of mainstream NGOs. Although Indego's revenue by the end of my research exceeded the $250,000 ceiling I imposed in the quantitative parts my analysis, I elected to retain it for the book, since its emergence mirrors that of other grassroots INGOs and because the ways in which it might develop into a more traditional NGO raise questions for further study.

What all of the organizations I ultimately selected had in common was the world region in which they operate. All five work in East Africa: one in a slum of Nairobi, Kenya; two in Rwanda, with most operations in the capital, Kigali; one in a large town in Uganda; and the last in a village thirty kilometers from a provincial capital in Tanzania. These four countries are among the most common destination countries for grassroots INGOs, with Kenya as the second-most-common country. The (relative) proximity of these organizations allowed me to spend a month in fall 2012 visiting these organizations, observing their projects, and talking with their staff and beneficiaries. During those visits most of the conversations were in English, but a few were in local languages (Swahili or Kinyarwanda) translated on the spot into English by a native speaker. During my short time with each organization, my goal was not assessing the impact of their work but rather getting a sense of the setting and the relative size and prominence of the grassroots INGO within the field of other development actors. I was able to see how professionalized each organization was: Were there shiny, air-conditioned offices or mud-brick buildings? Were the local employees or volunteers among the national elites? How did these local workers talk about their American colleagues and donors or short-term volunteers that came from the United States? How closely did my observations match the depictions of the grassroots INGO leaders back in the United States? This short-term fieldwork was part of the strategy of triangulating the story of grassroots INGOs.

While choosing one geographic region made fieldwork possible on a dissertation budget, it had the drawback of limiting my in-depth analysis to organizations in Africa. Political regimes, colonial trajectories, local resources, and language all vary geographically and shape the context in which NGOs function. My research strategy prevents me from speaking meaningfully to those differences in this book. Yet I found, to my surprise, that grassroots INGO leaders also have surprisingly little to say about the contextual specifics of where they work. Websites typically do not emphasize the historical or political particularities of grassroots INGOs' target countries; instead, narratives emphasize the serendipitous connections that brought the organization's founders to that certain place. In the interviews I found that American volunteers know little of the history or even the contemporary political circumstances of the places they work. In other words, although many Americans working with grassroots INGOs are not conscious of how place shapes their work, future research should do more to consider the influence of these contexts.

Codes Used in Content Analysis

Aid Context
civilized/developed/progressing
corrupt
destination country
ecological/economic conditions
past strife/disaster
poverty statistics

Role for Supporters
child sponsorship
goods solicited
US-based volunteer work solicited
money solicited
prayer solicited
invited to social media
volunteer work/visits abroad solicited

Project Sector
agriculture
animal husbandry
capacity building
Christian ministry
clean water source

cultural exchange
democracy building/politics
disaster relief
education (any)
education-scholarships
education-build schools
family planning/women's health
feeding/food distribution
loans/microcredit
medical supplies/local clinics
medical teams
orphanage
research
small business/microenterprise
sports
support cultural heritage

Partner Org
artists or arts orgs
business donors
business partners (non-retail, non-donor)
cooperatives
receiving-country government
foundation donors
immigrant/diaspora org
INGO
receiving-country congregation
receiving-country NGO
org has affiliates outside US
other US chapter
retail partners
Peace Corps
Rotary Club
US congregation
US government (any level or agency)

US K-12 school
US university

Photo
American volunteer
landscape
local child(ren)
local man
local women
recipients happy
recipients suffering
recipients working
religious symbol

Rationale
epidemic disease
gender inequality
God's purposes
human rights
justice
natural disaster
oppression by outsiders
political strife
refer to authority of international org (WHO, UNDP, etc.)
refer to scientific authority
small world/interdependence
suffering
war

Recipient
childlike or naive
children/youth
disabled
elderly
families

future ambitions
hardworking
kind/good/hospitable
living in deprived conditions
men
orphans
personal story
referred to by work role
shared humanity
vulnerable
women

Volunteer/Staff
holds BA or higher
Christian
immigrant
working in memory of loved one
link to aid-receiving country through adoption
non-immigrant in immigrant-founded org
previous global voluntarism or travel
serendipitous meeting w/ local(ity)
working with spouse/partner/child

Grassroots International NGOs in Website Sample

Name	Aid Model	City and State
A Touch of Love Foundation	Goods and Services	Ventura, CA
Abandoned Little Angels-Nhom Tinh Thuong	Goods and Services	Houston, TX
Able & Willing International Education Foundation, Inc.	Skills and Dispositions	Jefferson, MD
Abraham's Tent	Goods and Services	East Meadow, NY
Afghanistan Relief Organization	Goods and Services	Cypress, CA
Africa Community Exchange	Skills and Dispositions	Midlothian, VA
African Education and Leadership Initiative	Skills and Dispositions	Knoxville, TN
Africa Hope	Goods and Services	Dacula, GA
Africa in Mind, Inc.	Skills and Dispositions	Concord, CA
Alternative Medicine Intl	Goods and Services	Bakersfield, CA
Amazon Partnerships Foundation	Social Relations	Bothell, WA
American Program for Educational Enhancement in Developing Countries	Skills and Dispositions	Silver Spring, MD
Andando Foundation	Goods and Services	Eugene, OR
Antahkarana	Social Relations	Bozeman, MT
Africa Resurrection and Restoration Ministries	Skills and Dispositions	Chicago, IL

(continued)

Name	Aid Model	City and State
Baobei Foundation	Goods and Services	Ann Arbor, MI
Barrels of Love, Inc.	Goods and Services	Birmingham, AL
Beatitudes, Inc.	Skills and Dispositions	Little Rock, AR
BFA Library Project	Goods and Services	St Louis, MO
Bharathi Theertha	Goods and Services	Naperville, IL
Blue Marble Dreams, Inc.	Skills and Dispositions	Brooklyn, NY
Branches of the Vine	Goods and Services	Mason, OH
Cabeceras Aid Project	Social Relations	Houston, TX
Cafe Femenino Foundation	Skills and Dispositions	Vancouver, WA
Capacitar, Inc.	Skills and Dispositions	Santa Cruz, CA
Catholic League for the Poor of Nigeria	Goods and Services	Danville, IL
Central African Republic Renaissance Foundation, Inc.	Goods and Services	Fort Irwin, CA
Children's Opportunity Foundation	Goods and Services	Waterville, MN
Christian Dominican Medical Missions	Goods and Services	Summerville, SC
Circle of Hope International	Skills and Dispositions	Wilmore, KY
Congo Global Action	Social Relations	Chicago, IL
Connecting Connection	Goods and Services	Red Wing, MN
Cotton Tree Foundation, Inc.	Skills and Dispositions	Nashville, TN
Crimes of War Education Project	Social Relations	Washington, DC
Croi	Goods and Services	Bedford, TX
Cuban-American Military Council	Social Relations	Miami, FL
Cunningham Foundation	Goods and Services	Englewood, CO
Eco Africa Social Ventures, Inc.	Skills and Dispositions	New York, NY
Educating Africans for Christ	Skills and Dispositions	Jackson, MS
Education for Hope	Skills and Dispositions	Woodbridge, VA
Families in Vietnam	Goods and Services	Leander, TX
Financiers Without Borders	Skills and Dispositions	New York, NY
Flagstaff International Relief Effort	Goods and Services	Flagstaff, AZ
Fire of Life World Missions, Inc.	Skills and Dispositions	Fenton, MO

Forum for Information Technology Initiatives, Inc.	Goods and Services	Fort Washington, MD
Five for Water Foundation, Inc.	Goods and Services	Cape Girardeau, MO
Foundation for International Medicine	Goods and Services	Cincinnati, OH
Finding Freedom through Friendship	Goods and Services	Lexington, KY
Friends of Al-Rowwad USA, Inc.	Social Relations	Cambridge, MA
Friends of Rancho de Ninos	Goods and Services	Albuquerque, NM
Friends of UNIFAT	Skills and Dispositions	Bala Cynwyd, PA
Friends of Mukisa	Goods and Services	Philadelphia, PA
From God to Man	Goods and Services	Darby, PA
Fundacion Alma	Skills and Dispositions	New York, NY
Gambia Health Education Liaison Project (Help)	Skills and Dispositions	Seattle, WA
Global Connections Project	Goods and Services	Bloomington, MN
Global Environmental Relief Incorporated	Goods and Services	Conyers, GA
Global Justice Ecology Project	Social Relations	Hinesburg, VT
Global Passion Mission	Goods and Services	N. Fort Myers, FL
Global Routes	Social Relations	Northampton, MA
God's Grace Ministries NFP	Goods and Services	Matteson, IL
Going Beyond Borders	Goods and Services	Orem, UT
Golden Bridge Association, Inc.	Social Relations	Santa Barbara, CA
Graceworks Hope Network for Children International	Goods and Services	Anaheim, CA
Grandmothers Raising Grandchildren, Inc.	Goods and Services	Walnut Creek, CA
Great Peoples Foundation	Goods and Services	Brooklyn, NY
Grwks, Inc.	Goods and Services	Richardson, TX
Guyana Medical Relief	Goods and Services	Los Angeles, CA
Help Makwanpur Foundation	Goods and Services	West Point, PA
Henri Riquet Perpignand Foundation, Inc.	Goods and Services	W. Hempstead, NY
High Cloud Foundation	Goods and Services	Woodbridge, VA
Hope Charities, Inc.	Goods and Services	Portland, OR

(continued)

Name	Aid Model	City and State
Hope International Relief and Development Agency	Goods and Services	Columbus, OH
House on the Hill, Inc.	Skills and Dispositions	Okolona, MS
Howley Foundation	Goods and Services	South Burlington, VT
Human Dignity International	Social Relations	Casper, WY
Investours	Skills and Dispositions	Cambridge, MA
Irrigation Without Borders	Goods and Services	Woodstock, GA
Island Aid	Goods and Services	San Francisco, CA
Isuikwuato Progressive Union	Goods and Services	Dallas, TX
Join Together Society America	Goods and Services	New York, NY
Just Hope International (Know Think Act)	Goods and Services	Brentwood, TN
Kopernik Solutions	Goods and Services	New York, NY
Livingkindness Foundation	Skills and Dispositions	San Diego, CA
Macaya Foundation, Inc.	Goods and Services	Miramar, FL
Mats International, Inc.	Goods and Services	Richmond, IN
Medicine and Beyond	Goods and Services	Sacramento, CA
Mercy Airlift	Goods and Services	Los Angeles, CA
Mezzi Foundation, Inc.	Skills and Dispositions	Dorchester, MA
Minnesota Uruguay Partners Of The Americas	Social Relations	Minneapolis, MN
Missions of Grace	Goods and Services	San Antonio, TX
Mothers Fighting for Others, Inc.	Goods and Services	Santa Clarita, CA
Moving Windmills Project, Inc.	Skills and Dispositions	New York, NY
Myles of Great Hopes	Goods and Services	Cary, NC
Nechung Foundation	Social Relations	New York, NY
Nepal House Society - US Chapter, Inc.	Skills and Dispositions	Alpharetta, GA
Nagarathar Sangam of North America, Inc.	Social Relations	Monmouth Jct, NJ
OB Mexico, Inc.	Skills and Dispositions	Dallas, TX
OMID-USA	Goods and Services	Terrace Park, OH
Onemaker, Inc.	Skills and Dispositions	Edna, TX

OneSeventeen, Inc.	Goods and Services	Oklahoma City, OK
Open International	Skills and Dispositions	Arlington, VA
Opportunity Africa	Skills and Dispositions	Bemidji, MN
Our Responsibility, Inc.	Skills and Dispositions	Seal Beach, CA
Overseas Helping Hands	Skills and Dispositions	Portland, OR
Pathways Africa	Skills and Dispositions	Claremont, CA
Plumbers Without Borders	Goods and Services	Houston, TX
Pop's Foundation	Goods and Services	Acworth, GA
Power of One Ministry	Goods and Services	Charlotte, NC
Proyecto Bienestar	Skills and Dispositions	Branson, MO
Rainbow World Mission, Inc.	Goods and Services	Hackensack, NJ
Read for Kids Donate to Kids, Inc.	Goods and Services	Las Vegas, NV
Rebuild Southern Africa Association, Inc.	Goods and Services	Diablo, CA
Sahasra Deepika	Skills and Dispositions	Sterling, VA
San Alfonso Mission	Goods and Services	Broomfield, CO
7 Day Hero	Goods and Services	Santa Ana, CA
Shic Inc Asian Health Services Exchange	Goods and Services	Tulsa, OK
Shining City Foundation, Inc.	Goods and Services	Urbandale, IA
Soup by the Yard	Goods and Services	New Hope, VA
Sove Lavi	Goods and Services	Southlake, TX
Spirit of Sharing	Goods and Services	Colville, WA
St. David's Relief Foundation	Goods and Services	Mesquite, TX
Step of Faith Ministry, Inc.	Goods and Services	Bricktown, NJ
Suba Yo Foundation for Women And Children	Skills and Dispositions	New York, NY
Sustainable Collective Solutions, Inc.	Goods and Services	La Canada, CA
The Kilgoris Project	Skills and Dispositions	Los Altos, CA
The Rose International Fund	Goods and Services	Saratoga, CA
Threads of Hope Africa, Inc.	Skills and Dispositions	Tustin, CA
TMAGC, Inc.	Skills and Dispositions	Naperville, IL
Trans Africa Partners, Inc.	Goods and Services	Madison, AL
Udhyami Nepali	Skills and Dispositions	Astoria, NY
Uganda Hope Africa	Goods and Services	Yorkville, IL
Unite Foundation	Skills and Dispositions	Washington, DC

(continued)

Name	Aid Model	City and State
Village School Foundation	Skills and Dispositions	Bend, OR
Virtis, Inc.	Goods and Services	Carmichael, CA
Wallace Toronto Foundation	Social Relations	Salt Lake City, UT
Washington Kurdish Institute	Social Relations	Washington, DC
We R Love	Goods and Services	Middleburg, FL
Wells of Hope International, Inc.	Goods and Services	Conyers, GA
Weniruda Enterprise	Skills and Dispositions	Nashville, TN
What Better Looks Like	Skills and Dispositions	West Hempstead, NY
White Dove Foundation	Skills and Dispositions	Burnsville, MN
Wings of Peace	Goods and Services	Winter Spring, FL
Women Work Together	Social Relations	Boulder, CO
Women's Entrepreneurship Initiative	Skills and Dispositions	Scottsdale, AZ
World Birth Aid	Goods and Services	Seattle, WA
Young Heroes Foundation	Goods and Services	New York, NY
Youth 4 The Kingdom, A Non Profit Corporation	Goods and Services	Phoenix, AZ
Yspaniola Incorporated	Skills and Dispositions	San Francisco, CA

Notes

Introduction

1. Giving USA 2017, 2018.

2. Calculated from 2012 Business Master File (BMF) of public charities from the IRS, using organizations labeled as International Relief, Development, or Human Rights organizations (NTEE-CC codes Q30–39 and Q70). The international aid organizations depicted in figure 1 are also those with these codes. See appendix 1, "Note on Methods," for more on the BMF and the classification of tax-exempt organizations using the NTEE-CC codes.

3. Jad 2010; Mosse 2011.

4. Contrast with the common practice of trickling aid funds through a chain of half a dozen aid groups that span several countries, as described in Swidler and Watkins 2008.

5. Forman and Stoddard 2002, p. 270.

6. Smith 1990, 1998.

7. Babb 2009.

8. Anheier and Salamon 1998.

9. But as Aksartova 2009 points out, funding nonprofit organizations is not tantamount to building a robust civil society. See also Hammack and Heydemann 2009.

10. Anheier and Salamon 2006.

11. Forman and Stoddard 2002.

12. OECD 2013.

13. Worthington 2013; OECD 2013.

14. World society theory also emphasizes a special cultural status for NGOs. This literature identifies three macro-cultural shifts since the mid-twentieth century that facilitated NGOs' rise: the tendency to channel social action through modern organizations, the widespread legitimacy of rational, scientific action, and the rise of the global as the relevant social horizon. See Boli and Thomas 1997; Drori, Meyer, and Hwang 2006; and Frank and Meyer 2007.

15. Hilhorst 2003, p. 7, quoted in Watkins, Swidler, and Hannan 2012, p. 290.

16. Edwards and Hulme 1996, p. 962.

17. Smith and Lipsky 1993; Jenkins 1998; Karl 1998; Skocpol 2003; Grønbjerg 1993; Putnam 2001.

18. Hwang and Powell 2009, p. 268.

19. Forman and Stoddard 2002, p. 264.

20. The discussion in this section refers mainly to NGOs based in the Global North but working in the South. Many Global South NGOs have also formalized and in many cases entered into contracting relationships with donors. Some critics see this not as professionalization, but as co-optation. See Biggs and Neame 1996; Farrington et al. 1993; and Fowler 2000. On contracts and grants to NGOs, see USAID, "Top 40 Vendors."

21. Agensky 2013, p. 471.

22. Mosse 2011, 2013.

23. World society scholars Meyer and Bromley (2013) observe a "blurring" between government, for-profit, and nonprofit sectors. Lancaster (2009) and Honig (2018) offer evidence of the rationalization and professionalization of government international development agencies.

24. Krause 2014.

25. I draw here on the definition of globalization from Held and McGrew 2010.

26. Bennet and Segerberg 2012; Skocpol 2003; Putnam 2001; Simon 2011.

27. Cohen (2004) argues that today's political consumer usually acts individually rather than collectively, and rarely confronts the state directly, in contrast to the unions and women's organizations that led many of the consumer movements of the early twentieth century.

28. While the Nike boycott was a grassroots movement, Oxfam UK devoted years to evaluating and scoring the social and environmental practices of

multinational corporations in its "Behind the Brands" campaign. See Bennet and Segerberg 2012.

29. Schmitz et al. 2019, p. 14.

30. The movement of volunteer-driven development aid isn't limited to the United States. A growing field of research examines volunteer aid groups based in other countries in the Global North. Kinsbergen, Schulpen, and colleagues have carried out national studies of Dutch organizations they call Private Development Initiatives. Fylkes, Haaland, and Wallevik have studied "citizen aid" work by Norwegian citizens, some of which happens under the aegis of formal organizations, and some of which is done ad hoc. Similar efforts have been documented in Wales and elsewhere in the United Kingdom. As Fetcher and Schwittay acknowledge in an introduction to collection of articles on volunteer-driven aid, what distinguishes these efforts is less their organizational form than their hands-on, citizen-to-citizen character. *Amateurs without Borders* is the first national study of such groups based in the United States. See Kinsbergen 2014; Kinsbergen and Schulpen 2011; Kinsbergen, Tolsma, and Ruiter 2013; Fylkesnes 2018; Haaland and Wallevik 2017; Clifford 2016; Fechter 2012; and Fechter and Schwittay 2019.

31. Korten 1987, 1990.

32. Lounsbury and Strang 2009.

33. Rose-Ackerman 1996; Chaves 1998.

34. Frumkin 2002.

35. Frumkin 2002.

36. Some analyses of the nonprofit sector categorize organizations as "service" or "expressive" depending on their main domain of activity. Organizations that provide education, health care, or social services are typically deemed "service" organizations, while culture, recreation, religion, advocacy, and civic activities are deemed "expressive." (See, e.g., Salamon et al. 2017. Note that Salamon's typology puts international activities into a residual "other" category.) For theoretical purposes I find Frumkin's approach of identifying instrumental and expressive rationales more useful; while one rationale might dominate in a domain or particular organization, the other rationale may often coexist and can animate some of the tensions within the organization. See, for example, Suarez 2010; Knutsen 2013.

37. Kristof 2010; Polman 2010.

38. Appadurai 1996, p. 23.

39. Mainstream INGOs struggle with accountability, as well; see Ebrahim 2003. The point I make here and elaborate in chapter 5 is that grassroots INGOs' small size and emphasis on personal relationships does not rescue them from accountability problems.

40. Some volunteers of grassroots INGOs are professionals in other domains, and, as I describe further on, they in fact prize the opportunity to share their occupational knowledge. But with rare exceptions—the political science professor or USAID veteran who moonlights on a grassroots INGO board—these individuals are amateurs in the world of development aid.

41. Salamon 1987.

42. Eitzen 1989.

43. I describe the data and research methods in detail in appendix 1, "Note on Methods."

44. For example, Ahmed and Potter 2006; Barr, Fafchamps, and Owens 2005; Brass 2012; Limoncelli 2016.

45. Watkins, Swidler, and Hannan 2012.

46. Elsewhere I use IRS data to analyze the US locations where grassroots INGOs are based; see Schnable 2015b.

47. Such umbrella organizations include Interaction, Accord Independent Sector, and state-level nonprofit associations. See Appe and Schnable 2019.

48. Saxton and Guo 2012.

49. The main limitation to this approach is selection bias: organizations without websites may differ somewhat in their programs from organizations with websites, but in the absence of a survey there is no way to be certain. As I describe in chapter 2, websites were located for 6,564 of 10,624 registered organizations, or 61 percent. In comparing groups with websites to those without on *known* quantities—that is, those in the IRS data—I found that groups with websites had higher average income and were older than groups without websites at statistically significant levels.

Chapter One

1. Mosse 2011; Oelberger 2019; Fechter 2012.

2. Muyinga is a pseudonym.

Chapter Two

1. Cf. Kinsbergen's descriptive statistics of Dutch Private Development Initiatives' budgets, founding years, number of supporters, and project characteristics based on a survey of 893 organizations. But note that organizations with up to twenty staff members and budgets of up to 1 million euros can be categorized as PDIs if they otherwise offer direct support to developing countries, are not funded by the Ministry of Foreign Affairs, and have a voluntary character. Kinsbergen 2014, p. 57.

2. I discuss the problem of selection bias in appendix 1.

3. Powell et al. 2016

4. I use the term *aid recipients* (and elsewhere *beneficiaries*) here deliberately. The issue of how to designate the people who benefit from aid is part of the larger questions about the role of those people within development projects and about their depiction by aid givers (a topic I take up in chapter 6). This chapter shows that grassroots INGOs vary in how they depict the people they aim to serve. While some depict those people as partners or refer to them in work roles (e.g., Indego Africa refers to "artisan partners" on its website), many grassroots INGOs depict them as something closer to clients. For me to use the language of "partners" or "coproduction," as some development scholars do, would inaccurately depict many grassroots INGOs. Who receives what in aid relationships is of course not simple; "aid givers" derive benefits from these relationships too, as the following chapters show. I thus use terms like *aid recipients* and *aid givers* in their least-common-denominator sense, and trust the reader to recognize that these roles and relationships are more complicated in reality.

5. Wuthnow 1991. Nina Eliasoph (2020) has argued that volunteers have multiple motives and that they interrogate their own motives and "argue with one another about which motive is really in play." She claims that while trying to pinpoint a "true" motive for volunteer action is futile, researchers can focus on what it is that is valued in the act of volunteering.

6. Organizations may work in more than one country and are coded for every country and region in which they work.

7. US Agency for International Development May 2019.

8. US Census Bureau; American Community Survey n.d. The surveys are broken down by region into separate tables.

9. Swidler and Watkins 2009.

10. The "fair trade" designation requires membership in the Fair Trade Federation, which screens retail and wholesale operations in North America, or the World Fair Trade Organization, which sets standards for production and sale of goods in all countries outside North America (Shorette 2014). Achieving accreditation from these groups is a demanding process, so some grassroots INGOs in this sample (including Indego Africa) opt out. The grassroots INGOs set above-market prices that, they argue, generate a living wage for producers. See as examples of this practice the grassroots INGOs Café Feminino, Five for Water, and Indego Africa.

11. Eade 2010; Moore 2001.

12. Clark 1991.

13. OECD 2018.

14. In a private conversation, the former CEO of an American INGO with annual revenues in the tens of millions conceded his personal frustrations with child sponsorship. He acknowledged that it reinforced racial stereotypes and conflicted with the organization's need for unrestricted donations. However, he admitted, it was a hugely effective fundraising tool, and he doubted that his former organization would ever abandon it.

15. Case study interviews revealed that even when these tasks are not advertised publicly, new organizations rely heavily on favors within personal networks to get these tasks done. Someone typically has an accountant or attorney friend that handles the registration paperwork to achieve 501(c)3 status, and someone else has a friend who can build a simple website.

Chapter Three

1. Deaton 2013.

2. Sen 1999.

3. See, for example, North 1990; Portes and Smith 2012; Rodrik 2006.

4. *Economist* 1958

5. World Development 1991. Watkins, Swidler, and Hannan 2012, p. 287

6. Watkins, Swidler, and Hannan 2012, p. 296.

7. Watkins, Swidler, and Hannan 2012, p. 299.

8. Korten 1990, p. 131.

9. Korten 1990.

10. "Career Opportunities in International Development" 2007.

11. Budiman and Lopez 2017.

12. US Travel and Tourism Statistics 2015.

13. Blake and Lande 1998.

14. The measure is cellular subscriptions per capita. This high rate is accounted for partly by the common practice of cell phone users having pay-as-you-go subscriptions on more than one network. See International Telecommunications Union 2014.

15. Western Union 2017.

16. Krause 2014.

17. Swidler and Watkins 2017, p. vii.

18. Deaton 2013.

Chapter Four

1. On the formal and informal ways that mainstream NGOs develop knowledge, see Oelberger 2019; Lewis and Mosse 2006.

2. Innocenti 2003; UNICEF South Asia n.d. See also a coalition of mainstream INGOs and other development actors that oppose institutional care for children: www.retthinkorphanages.org.

3. Compare with Lasker's (2016) research on short-term medical missions. Many partners in the aid-receiving countries cite the equipment and medication that the short-term volunteers bring as one of the useful benefits to the aid-receiving community (p. 131). Lasker's interviews with the American leaders of these organizations show that some are concerned about the long-term effects of directly providing goods and services in developing countries, such as the lack of continued patient care and the impediments to building local capacity.

4. Korten 1990, p. 119.

5. Keck and Sikkink 1998.

6. Partners of the Americas organizations have ties dating back to the Kennedy administration. Individual chapters were organized and registered with the IRS at different times, including this chapter, registered in 1991.

7. Swidler and Watkins 2017.

8. DeTemple 2020. DeTemple argues further that there were negative spillover effects to the failure of the cheese-making enterprise; the women became alienated from one another and from the religious organization that had helped nurture the project.

9. Cornwall and Brock 2005; Swidler and Watkins 2017

Chapter Five

1. Edwards and Hulme 1996; Banks, Hulme, and Edwards 2015.

2. Barr, Fafchamps, and Owens 2005.

3. Dupuy, Ron, and Prakash 2016.

4. Barr, Fafchamps, and Owens 2005; Watkins, Swidler, and Hannan 2012.

5. Leal 2010.

6. White 2011; Ebrahim 2003.

7. Mansuri and Rao 2012.

8. Krause 2014.

9. Based on an analysis of the 2010 IRS Business Master File; see appendix 1 on methods for details.

10. This is a conservative estimate. I coded grassroots INGO volunteers "working with family members" only when a family relationship was specifically mentioned on the website, typically in a board member's biography or an account of a trip to the aid-receiving community. As I describe below, spouses or parents/children worked together in four out of five case study NGOs; in the fifth, parents made financial contributions, but did not volunteer (since RUI accepted only MDs as volunteers abroad).

11. Appe and Oreg (2019) also found personal networks to be crucial to fundraising for a set of grassroots INGOs based in upstate New York.

12. Pseudonym substituted for Natalie's true name.

13. Child sponsorship programs impose huge administrative burdens for enrolling and tracking sponsored children and maintaining communication with their sponsors. But these costs typically pay off because sponsorships are a source of recurring, unrestricted income. See Bornstein 2001; Maren 1997; Plewes and Stuart 2007.

14. Wuthnow 2009.

15. Queenan, Allen, and Tuomala 2013.

16. Lewis and Mosse 2006.

17. Swidler 2009, p. 206.

18. Lewis and Mosse 2006.

19. Watkins, Swidler, and Hannan 2012; Swidler and Watkins 2017.

20. Swidler and Watkins 2009; Frye (2012) similarly describes Malawian schoolgirls' aspirations to be educated, modern subjects, even when the economic gains from more education are likely to be nil.

21. Baccarini 1999.

22. Ebrahim 2003, p. 203.

23. Swidler and Watkins 2017.

24. Ebrahim 2003, p. 197.

25. Fry 1995.

Chapter Six

1. Dryzek and Niemeyer 2008, p. 481.

2. Dryzek and Niemeyer 2008, p. 482.

3. Critical scholarship scrutinizes development discourse on the grounds that it constitutes and maintains the power of the Global North. While I recognize the powerful ability of discourse to shape cognition, I follow Rubenstein's (2015) claim that INGO discourse need not reinforce existing relations of power.

4. Rubenstein 2015, p. 182.

5. Rosario 2003.

6. Lamers 2005.

7. Cameron and Haanstra 2008.

8. Plewes and Stuart 2007; Dogra 2007.

9. Cameron and Haanstra 2008, p. 1478.

10. Cameron and Haanstra 2008.

11. Rubenstein 2015, p. 73.

12. Rubenstein 2015, p. 182.

13. Rubenstein 2015, p. 192.

Chapter Seven

1. Swidler 2001.

2. Bender 2003; Chaves 2010; Smilde 2007.

3. Smith 1990, p. 50.

4. Kniss and Campbell 1997.

5. Agensky 2013; Bornstein 2001; Burchardt 2013.

6. Chaves 2010.

7. Swidler 1986, 2001; Wuthnow 1996; DiMaggio 1997. For a competing view of culture in which values guide human behavior in relatively consistent ways, see Vaisey 2009.

8. Becker and Dhingra 2001; Bekkers and Schuyt 2008; Musick and Wilson 2008; Putnam and Campbell 2010; Schnable 2015a.

9. Cornwell and Harrison 2004.

10. Miller and Yamamori 2007; Wuthnow 2009; Offutt 2015.

11. Probasco 2013; Ver Beek 2006; Wuthnow 2009; Lasker 2016; Lough et al. 2011.

12. Ver Beek 2006

13. Pattillo-McCoy 1998.

14. Snow and Benford 1988, 1992; Goffman 1974.

15. Ferguson 1994; Frank and Meyer 2007; Schnable et al. 2020

16. Small, Harding, and Lamont 2010, p. 14

17. John 7:37–38

18. Bender 2003; Hall 1997; Kurien 2007; Mahmood 2005; Orsi 1996.

19. Jenkins 2002; Levitt 2001, 2007; Miller and Yamamori 2007; Offutt 2015; Wuthnow and Offutt 2008.

20. Wuthnow 2009, p. 91.

21. Pew Research Center, Global Attitudes and Trends, 2011–2013.

Conclusion

1. Skocpol 2003.

2. Lancaster 2007.

3. Hwang and Powell 2009.

4. Halliday et al. 1987; DiMaggio 2006.

5. With four of the case study organizations persisting at $250,000 or less and one exceeding that budget, these groups have fared slightly better over time than the population of grassroots INGOs recorded in IRS records. At the end of 2011, 8,294 active organizations met the criteria for grassroots international NGOs: they were founded in 1990 or later and had an annual budget of

$250,000 or less. Five year later, 67 percent of those organizations still met those criteria. Six hundred twelve, or roughly 7 percent, had grown past the $250,000 threshold. But the remaining 26 percent were no longer active in IRS records. At the time of this writing, in late 2019, an additional 250 organizations that had been active in 2016 were gone (although 58 had come back from the dead). One hundred sixty-one had graduated from grassroots status since 2016. Thus, of the 8,294 grassroots international NGOs active at the end of 2011, 64 percent of them persisted at grassroots status seven and a half years later. Note, though, that the IRS practice of not recording revenue less than $50,000 per year makes it possible for organizations to maintain a presence on paper even if they have not carried out any work in a given year. Future research might look more closely at the death or dormancy of grassroots INGOs.

6. Eliasoph 2011, p. 120.

7. Ferguson 1994.

8. Innocenti 2003; UNICEF South Asia, n.d. See also rethinkorphanges.org.

9. For example, Mercer 2003; White 2011; Mercelis et al. 2016.

Appendix One

1. Appe and Schnable 2019.

2. For example, Beckfield 2003; Boli and Thomas 1997; Frank 1997. This publication has the advantages of historical recognition by the UN (Boli and Thomas 1997) and data on organizations' members and operating locations. While it covers international organizations for a range of purposes—industry, science, and sports groups are dominant—the *Yearbook*'s shortcoming is that it defines "international" organizations as only those operating in three or more countries. The *Yearbook* excludes most of the US-based aid organizations recognized by the IRS.

3. Ahmed and Potter 2006; Brass 2012; Barr et al. 2005.

4. Historically the most common beneficiaries of this "full subsidiary" rule have been parochial schools. Although they are not required to do so, many religious congregations register with the IRS; in 2003, the BMF included one hundred thirty thousand religious congregations, or about one-third of the total estimated number of congregations in the United States.

5. The National Center for Charitable Statistics at the Urban Institute took the leading role in developing NTEE codes and making them accessible

to researchers and the public. I use the NTEE-CC codes here; Foundation Center uses a slightly modified version of the NTEE system in its records. See Jones 2019.

6. NTEE-CC Manual 2007, p. 138.

7. Amazon Mechanical Turk is a clearinghouse to outsource large numbers of small tasks that require human intelligence. For an overview, see https://www.mturk.com/worker/help. For a discussion of the quality of data generated with Mechanical Turk, see Kittur et al. 2008.

8. Blei et al. 2003.

9. Schnable 2016.

10. Schnable 2015b.

11. A 501(c)3 organization with less than $25,000 in revenue was not required to report an exact amount to the IRS with its annual Form 990-N filing though the end of 2010, This was the case for the records of most organizations here. Their revenues are recorded by the IRS as $0.

Bibliography

Agensky, Jonathan C. "Dr Livingstone, I Presume? Evangelicals, Africa and Faith-Based Humanitarianism." *Global Society* 27, no. 4 (2013): 454–74. https://doi.org/10.1080/13600826.2013.823916.

Ahmed, Shamima, and David M. Potter. *NGOs in International Politics.* Bloomfield, CT: Kumarian Press, 2006.

Aksartova, Sada. "Promoting Civil Society or Diffusing NGOs? U.S. Donors in the Former Soviet Union." In *Globalization, Philanthropy, and Civil Society: Projecting Institutional Logics Abroad*, edited by David C. Hammack and Steven Heydemann, 160–91. Bloomington: Indiana University Press, 2009.

Anheier, Helmut K., and Lester M. Salamon, editors. *The Nonprofit Sector in the Developing World: A Comparative Analysis.* Manchester: Manchester University Press, 1998.

———. "The Nonprofit Sector in Comparative Perspective." In *The Nonprofit Sector: A Research Handbook*, 2nd edition, edited by Walter W. Powell and Richard Steinberg, 89–116. New Haven, CT: Yale University Press, 2006.

Appadurai, Arjun. *Modernity at Large: Cultural Dimensions of Globalization.* Minneapolis: University of Minnesota Press, 1996.

Appe, Susan, and Ayelet Oreg. "Lost and Found in Upstate New York: Exploring the Motivations of "'Lost Boys'" Refugees as Founders of International Nonprofit Organizations." *Administration & Society* (2019): 0095399719890311.

Appe, Susan, and Allison Schnable. "Don't Reinvent the Wheel: Possibilities for and Limits to Building Capacity of Grassroots International NGOs." *Third World Quarterly* 40, no. 10 (2019): 1832–49.

Babb, Sarah. *Behind the Development Banks: Washington Politics, World Poverty, and the Wealth of Nations*. Chicago: University of Chicago Press, 2009.

Baccarini, David. "The Logical Framework Method for Defining Project Success." *Project Management Journal* 30, no. 4 (December 1999): 25-32. https://doi.org/10.1177/875697289903000405.

Banks, Nicola, David Hulme, and Michael Edwards. "NGOs, States, and Donors Revisited: Still Too Close for Comfort?" *World Development* 66 (February 2015): 707-18. https://doi.org/10.1016/j.worlddev.2014.09.028.

Barr, Abigail, Marcel Fafchamps, and Trudy Owens. "The Governance of Non-Governmental Organizations in Uganda." *World Development* 33, no. 4 (April 2005): 657-79. https://doi.org/10.1016/j.worlddev.2004.09.010.

Becker, Penny Edgell, and Pawan H. Dhingra. "Religious Involvement and Volunteering: Implications for Civil Society." *Sociology of Religion* 62, no. 3 (2001): 315. https://doi.org/10.2307/3712353.

Beckfield, Jason. "Inequality in the World Polity: The Structure of International Organization." *American Sociological Review*, 2003, 401-24.

Bekkers, René, and Theo Schuyt. "And Who Is Your Neighbor? Explaining Denominational Differences in Charitable Giving and Volunteering in the Netherlands." *Review of Religious Research* 50, no. 1 (September 2008): 74-96.

Bender, Courtney. *Heaven's Kitchen: Living Religion at God's Love We Deliver*. Chicago: University of Chicago Press, 2003.

Bennett, W. Lance, and Alexandra Segerberg. "The Logic of Connective Action: Digital Media and the Personalization of Contentious Politics." *Information, Communication & Society* 15, no. 5 (April 10, 2012): 739-98. https://doi.org/10.1080/1369118X.2012.670661.

Biggs, Stephen D., and Arthur D. Neame. "Negotiating Room to Maneuver: Reflections Concerning NGO Autonomy and Accountability with the New Policy Agenda." In *Beyond the Magic Bullet: NGO Performance and Accountability in the Post-Cold War World*, edited by Michael Edwards and David Hulme, 40-52. West Hartford, CT: Kumarian, 1996.

Blake, Linda, and Jim Lande. "Trends in the US International Telecommunications Industry." Industry Analysis Division: Common Carrier Bureau: Federal Communications Commission, August 1998. https://transition.fcc.gov/Bureaus/Common_Carrier/Reports/FCC-State_Link/Intl/itltrd98.pdf.

Blei, David. M., Andrew Y. Ng, and Michael I. Jordan. "Latent Dirichlet Allocation." *Journal of Machine Learning Research* 3 (2003): 993–1022.

Boli, John, and George M. Thomas. "World Culture in the World Polity: A Century of International Non-Governmental Organization." *American Sociological Review* 62, no. 2 (April 1997): 171–90. https://doi.org/10.2307/2657298.

Bornstein, Erica. "Child Sponsorship, Evangelism, and Belonging in the Work of World Vision Zimbabwe." *Journal of the American Ethnological Society* 28, no. 3 (August 2001): 595–622. https://doi.org/10.1525/ae.2001.28.3.595.

Brass, Jennifer. N. "Why Do NGOs Go Where They Go? Evidence from Kenya." *World Development* 40, no. 2 (2012): 387–401.

Budiman, Abby, and Mark Hugo Lopez. "Amid Decline in International Adoptions to U.S., Boys Outnumber Girls for the First Time." Pew Research Center, October 17, 2017. http://www.pewresearch.org/fact-tank/2017/10/17/amid-decline-in-international-adoptions-to-u-s-boys-outnumber-girls-for-the-first-time/.

Burchardt, Marian. "Faith-Based Humanitarianism: Organizational Change and Everyday Meanings in South Africa." *Sociology of Religion* 74, no. 1 (March 1, 2013): 30–55. https://doi.org/10.1093/socrel/srs068.

Cameron, John, and Anna Haanstra. 2008. "Development Made Sexy: How It Happened and What It Means." *Third World Quarterly* 29 (8): 1475–89. https://doi.org/10.1080/01436590802528564.

"Career Opportunities in International Development." Columbia University School of International and Public Affairs Office of Career Services, August 7, 2007.

Chaves, Mark. "The Religious Ethic and the Spirit of Entrepreneurialism." In *Private Action and the Public Good*, edited by W. W. Powell and Elisabeth Clemens, 20–35. New Haven, CT: Yale University Press, 1998.

———. "SSSR Presidential Address. Rain Dances in the Dry Season: Overcoming the Religious Congruence Fallacy." *Journal for the Scientific Study of Religion* 49, no. 1 (March 2010): 1–14. https://doi.org/10.1111/j.1468-5906.2009.01489.x.

Clark, John. *Democratizing Development: The Role of Voluntary Organizations*. West Hartford, CT: Kumarian, 1991.

Clifford, David. "International Charitable Connections: The Growth in Number, and the Countries of Operation, of English and Welsh Charities

Working Overseas." *Journal of Social Policy* 45, no. 3 (July 2016): 453–86. https://doi.org/10.1017/S0047279416000076.

Cohen, Lizabeth. "Consumers' Republic: The Politics of Mass Consumption in America." *Journal of Consumer Research* 31, no. 1 (June 1, 2004): 236–39. https://doi.org/10.1086/383439.

Cornwall, Andrea, and Karen Brock. "What Do Buzzwords Do for Development Policy? A Critical Look at 'Participation,' 'Empowerment' and 'Poverty Reduction.'" *Third World Quarterly* 26, no. 7 (2005): 1043–60.

Cornwell, Benjamin, and Jill Ann Harrison. "Union Members and Voluntary Associations: Membership Overlap as a Case of Organizational Embeddedness." *American Sociological Review* 69, no. 6 (December 2004): 862–81. https://doi.org/10.1177/000312240406900606.

Deaton, Angus. *The Great Escape: Health, Wealth, and the Origins of Inequality.* Princeton, NJ: Princeton University Press, 2013.

DiMaggio, Paul. "Culture and Cognition." *Annual Review of Sociology* 23, no. 1 (August 1997): 263–87. https://doi.org/10.1146/annurev.soc.23 .1.263.

———. "Nonprofit Organizations and the Intersectoral Division of Labor in the Arts." In *The Nonprofit Sector: A Research Handbook*, 2nd Edition, edited by Walter W. Powell and Richard Steinberg. New Haven, CT: Yale University Press, 2006.

Drori, Gili S., John W. Meyer, and Hokyu Hwang, eds. *Globalization and Organization: World Society and Organizational Change.* New York: Oxford University Press, 2006.

Dryzek, John S., and Simon Niemeyer. 2008. "Discursive Representation." *American Political Science Review* 102 (4): 481–93. https://doi.org/10.1017 /S0003055408080325.

Dupuy, Kendra, James Ron, and Aseem Prakash. "Hands Off My Regime! Governments' Restrictions on Foreign Aid to Non-Governmental Organizations in Poor and Middle-Income Countries." *World Development* 84 (August 2016): 299–311. https://doi.org/10.1016/j.worlddev.2016.02.001.

Eade, Deborah. "Capacity Building: Who Builds Whose Capacity." In *Deconstructing Development Discourse: Buzzwords and Fuzzwords*, edited by Andrea Cornwall and Deborah Eade, 148–57. Rugby, UK: Practical Action Publishing, 2010.

Ebrahim, Alnoor. "Making Sense of Accountability: Conceptual Perspectives for Northern and Southern Nonprofits." *Nonprofit Management & Leadership* 14, no. 2 (December 5, 2003): 191–212. https://doi.org/10.1002/nml.29.

Economist. "Private Versus Public Giving." December 27, 1958.

Edwards, Michael, and David Hulme. "Too Close for Comfort? The Impact of Official Aid on Nongovernmental Organizations." *World Development* 26, no. 6 (June 1996): 961–73. https://doi.org/10.1016/0305-750X(96)00019-8.

Eitzen, D. Stanley. "The Sociology of Amateur Sport: An Overview." *International Review for the Sociology of Sport* 24, no. 2 (1989): 95–105.

Eliasoph, Nina. *Making Volunteers.* Princeton, NJ: Princeton University Press, 2011.

———. "What Do Volunteers Do?" In *The Nonprofit Sector: A Research Handbook, 3rd Edition,* edited by Walter W. Powell and Patricia Bromley. Palo Alto, CA: Stanford University Press, 2020.

Farrington, John, Anthony Bebbington, Kate Wellard, and David J. Lewis. *Reluctant Partners? Nongovernmental Organizations, the State and Sustainable Agricultural Development.* London: Routledge, 1993.

Fechter, Anne-Meike. "The Personal and the Professional: Aid Workers' Relationships and Values in the Development Process." *Third World Quarterly* 33, no. 8 (September 2012): 1387–404. https://doi.org/10.1080/01436597.2012.698104.

Fechter, Anne-Meike, and Anke Schwittay. "Citizen Aid: Grassroots Interventions in Development and Humanitarianism." *Third World Quarterly* 40, no. 10 (2019): 1769–80.

Ferguson, James. *The Anti-Politics Machine: "Development," Depoliticization, and Bureaucratic Power in Lesotho.* Minneapolis: University of Minnesota Press, 1994.

Forman, Shepard, and Abby Stoddard. "International Assistance." In *The State of Nonprofit America,* edited by Lester Salamon, 240–70. Washington, DC: The Brookings Institution, 2002.

Fowler, Alan. "NGDOs as a Moment in History: Beyond Aid to Social Entrepreneurship or Civic Innovation?" *Third World Quarterly* 21, no. 4 (August 1, 2000): 637–54. https://doi.org/10.1080/713701063.

Frank, David John. "Science, Nature, and the Globalization of the Environment, 1870-1990." Social Forces 76, no. 2 (1997): 409–35.

Frank, David John, and John W. Meyer. "University Expansion and the Knowledge Society." *Theory and Society* 36, no. 4 (2007): 287–311.

Frumkin, Peter. *On Being Nonprofit: A Conceptual and Policy Primer*. Cambridge, MA: Harvard University Press, 2009.

Fry, Ronald E. "Accountability in Organizational Life: Problem or Opportunity for Nonprofits?" *Nonprofit Management and Leadership* 6, no. 2 (Winter 1995): 181–95. https://doi.org/10.1002/nml.4130060207.

Frye, Margaret. "Bright Futures in Malawi's New Dawn: Educational Aspirations as Assertions of Identity." *American Journal of Sociology* 117, no. 6 (May 2012): 1565–624. https://doi.org/10.1086/664542.

Fylkesnes, June. "Motivations behind Citizen Aid: Norwegian Initiatives in the Gambia." *Third World Quarterly* 40, no. 10 (2019): 1799–815.

Giving USA. *Giving USA: The Annual Report on Philanthropy for the Year 2016*. Chicago: Giving USA Foundation, 2017.

———. *Giving USA: The Annual Report on Philanthropy for the Year 2017*. Chicago: Giving USA Foundation, 2018.

Goffman, Erving. *Frame Analysis: An Essay on the Organization of Experience*. Cambridge, MA: Harvard University Press, 1974.

Grønbjerg, Kirsten A. *Understanding Nonprofit Funding: Managing Revenues in Social Services and Community Development Organizations*. San Francisco: Jossey-Bass, 1993.

Haaland, Hanne, and Hege Wallevik. "Citizens as Actors in the Development Field: The Case of an Accidental Aid-Agent's Activities in Aid-Land." *Forum for Development Studies* 44, no. 2 (May 4, 2017): 203–22. https://doi.org/10.1080/08039410.2017.1305444.

Hall, David D., ed. *Lived Religion in America: Toward a History of Practice*. Princeton, NJ: Princeton University Press, 1997.

Halliday, Terence C., Michael J. Powell, and Mark W. Granfors. "Minimalist Organizations: Vital Events in State Bar Associations, 1870–1930." *American Sociological Review* 52, no. 4 (1987): 456–71. https://doi.org/10.2307/2095291.

Hammack, David C., and Steven Heydemann, eds. "Philanthropic Projections: Sending Institutional Logics Abroad." In *Globalization, Philanthropy, and Civil Society: Projecting Institutional Logics Abroad*. Bloomington: Indiana University Press, 2009.

Held, David, and McGrew, Anthony. "The Great Globalization Debate: An Introduction." In *The Global Transformations Reader*, 2nd ed., 1–50. Cambridge: Polity, 2010.

Hilhorst, Dorothea. *The Real World of NGOs: Discourses, Diversity, and Development*. London; New York: Zed Books, 2003.

Honig, Dan. *Navigation by Judgment: Why and When Top-Down Management of Foreign Aid Doesn't Work*. New York: Oxford University Press, 2018.

Hwang, Hokyu, and Walter W. Powell. "The Rationalization of Charity: The Influences of Professionalism in the Nonprofit Sector." *Administrative Sciences Quarterly* 54 (2009): 268–98.

Innocenti, UNICEF Office of Research. "Children in Institutions: The Beginning of the End?" UNICEF-IRC, 2003. Accessed August 7, 2019. https://www.unicef-irc.org/publications/349-children-in-institutions-the-beginning-of-the-end.html.

International Telecommunications Union. "The World in 2014: Facts and Figures." Geneva: International Telecommunications Union, April 2014. https://www.itu.int/en/ITU-D/Statistics/Documents/facts/ICTFacts Figures2014-e.pdf.

Jad, Islah. "NGOs: Between Buzzwords and Social Movements." In *Deconstructing Development Discourse: Buzzwords and Fuzzwords*, edited by Andrea Cornwall and Deborah Eade, 167–93. Warwickshir, UK: Practical Action Publishing, 2010.

Jenkins, Jennifer C. "Channeling Social Protest: Foundation Patronage of Contemporary Social Movements." In *Private Action and the Public Good*, edited by W. W. Powell and Elisabeth Clemens, 206–16. New Haven, CT: Yale University Press, 1998.

Jenkins, Philip. *The Next Christendom: The Rise of Global Christianity*. New York: Oxford University Press, 2002.

Jones, Deondre. "National Taxonomy of Exempt Entities (NTEE) Codes." April 2, 2019. Accessed July 15, 2019. https://nccs.urban.org/project /national-taxonomy-exempt-entities-ntee-codes.

Karl, Barry D. "Volunteers and Professionals: Many Histories, Many Meanings." In *Private Action and the Public Good*, edited by W. W. Powell and Elisabeth Clemens, 245–57. New Haven, CT: Yale University Press, 1998.

Karpf, David. *Analytic Activism: Digital Listening and the New Political Strategy*. Oxford: Oxford University Press, 2016.

Keck, Margaret E., and Kathryn Sikkink. *Activism Beyond Borders: Advocacy Networks in International Politics*. Ithaca, NY: Cornell University Press, 1998.

Kinsbergen, Sara. *Behind the Pictures: Understanding Private Development Initiatives*. Nijmegen: Radbound University, 2014.

Kinsbergen, Sara, and Lau W. M. Schulpen. *The Netherlands Yearbook on International Cooperation 2009*. Assen: Van Gorcum & Comp. b.v., 2011.

Kinsbergen, Sara, Jochem Tolsma, and Stijn Ruiter. "Bringing the Beneficiary Closer: Explanations for Volunteering Time in Dutch Private Development Initiatives." *Nonprofit and Voluntary Sector Quarterly* 42, no. 1 (February 2013): 59–83. https://doi.org/10.1177/0899764011431610.

Kittur, Aniket, Ed H. Chi, and Bongwon Suh. "Crowdsourcing User Studies with Mechanical Turk." *Proceedings of the SIGCHI Conference on Human Factors in Computing Systems*, 2008, 453–56.

Kniss, Fred, and David Todd Campbell. "The Effect of Religious Orientation on International Relief and Development Organizations." *Journal for the Scientific Study of Religion* 36, no. 1 (March 1997): 93–103. https://doi.org/10.2307/1387885.

Knutsen, Wenjue Lu. "Value as a Self-Sustaining Mechanism: Why Some Nonprofit Organizations Are Different From and Similar to Private and Public Organizations." *Nonprofit and Voluntary Sector Quarterly* 42, no. 5 (2013): 985–1005.

Korten, David C. "Third Generation NGO Strategies: A Key to People-Centered Development." *World Development* 15 (September 1, 1987): 145–59. https://doi.org/10.1016/0305-750X(87)90153-7.

———. *Getting to the 21st Century: Voluntary Action and the Global Agenda*. West Hartford, CT: Kumarian Press, 1990.

Krause, Monika. *The Good Project: Humanitarian Relief NGOs and the Fragmentation of Reason*. Chicago: University of Chicago Press, 2014.

Kristof, Nicholas. "The D.I.Y. Foreign-Aid Revolution." *New York Times*, October 20, 2010, sec. Magazine.https://www.nytimes.com/2010/10/24/magazine/24volunteerism-t.html.

Kurien, Prema A. *A Place at the Multicultural Table: The Development of an American Hinduism*. New Brunswick, NJ: Rutgers Univ. Press, 2007.

Lamers, Machiel. "Representing Poverty, Impoverishing Representation? A Discursive Analysis of a NGOs Fundraising Posters." *Graduate Journal of Social Science* 2, no. 1 (2005): 37–74.

Lancaster, Carol. *Foreign Aid: Diplomacy, Development, Domestic Politics.* Chicago: University of Chicago Press, 2007.

Lasker, Judith N. *Hoping to Help: The Promises and Pitfalls of Global Health Volunteering.* Ithaca, NY: Cornell University Press, 2016.

Leal, Pablo Alejandro. "Participation: The Ascendancy of a Buzzword in the Neo-Liberal Era." *Development in Practice* 17, no. 4–5 (November 18, 2010): 539–48. https://doi.org/10.1080/09614520701469518.

Levitt, Peggy. *The Transnational Villagers.* Berkeley: University of California Press, 2001.

———. *God Needs No Passport: Immigrants and the Changing American Religious Landscape.* New York: New Press : Distributed by W.W. Norton & Company, 2007.

Lewis, David, and David Mosse, eds. *Development Brokers and Translators: The Ethnography of Aid and Agencies.* Bloomfield, CT: Kumarian Press, 2006.

Limoncelli, Stephanie A. "What in the World Are Anti-trafficking NGOs Doing? Findings from a Global Study." *Journal of Human Trafficking* 2, no. 4 (2016): 316–28.

Lough, Benjamin J., Amanda Moore McBride, Margaret S. Sherraden, and Kathleen O'Hara. "Capacity Building Contributions of Short-Term International Volunteers." *Journal of Community Practice* 19, no. 2 (April 2011): 120–37. https://doi.org/10.1080/10705422.2011.568921.

Lounsbury, Michael, and David Strang. "Social Entrepreneurship: Success Stories and Logic Construction." In *Globalization, Philanthropy, and Civil Society: Projecting Institutional Logics Abroad*, 71–94. Bloomington: Indiana University Press, 2009.

Mahmood, Saba. *Politics of Piety: The Islamic Revival and the Feminist Subject.* Princeton, NJ: Princeton University Press, 2005.

Mansuri, Ghazala, and Vijayendra Rao. *Localizing Development: Does Participation Work?* Washington, DC: The World Bank, 2012. https://doi.org/10.1596/978-0-8213-8256-1.

Maren, Michael. *The Road to Hell: The Ravaging Effects of Foreign Aid and International Charity.* New York: The Free Press, 1997.

Mercelis, Fleur, Lore Wellens, and Marc Jegers. "Beneficiary Participation in
Non-Governmental Development Organisations: A Case Study in Vietnam."
The Journal of Development Studies 52, no. 10 (2016)-:1446–62. doi:
10.1080/00220388.2016.1166209.

Mercer, Claire. 2003. "Performing Partnership: Civil Society and the Illusions
of Good Governance in Tanzania." *Political Geography* 22 (2003):741–63.

Meyer, John W., John Boli, George M. Thomas, and Francisco O. Ramirez.
"World Society and the Nation-State." *American Journal of Sociology* 103,
no. 1 (July 1997): 144–81. https://doi.org/10.1086/231174.

Meyer, John W., and Patricia Bromley. "The Worldwide Expansion of
'Organization.'" *Sociological Theory* 31, no. 4 (2013): 366–89.

Miller, Donald E., and Tetsunao Yamamori. *Global Pentecostalism: The New
Face of Christian Social Engagement.* Berkeley: University of California
Press, 2007.

Moore, Mick. "Empowerment at Last?" *Journal of International Development*
13, no. 3 (2001): 321–29.

Mosse, David. *Adventures in Aidland: The Anthropology of Professionals in International Development.* New York: Berghahn Books, 2011.

———. "The Anthropology of International Development." *Annual Review of
Anthropology* 42 (2013): 227–46.

Musick, Marc A., and John Wilson. *Volunteers: A Social Profile.* Bloomington:
Indiana University Press, 2008.

North, Douglass C. *Institutions, Institutional Change and Economic Performance.* Cambridge: Cambridge University Press, 1990.

OECD (Organisation for Economic Cooperation and Development). "Aid at a
Glance: Flows of Official Development Assistance to and through Civil
Society Organisations in 2011." Paris: OECD-Development Co-operation
Directorate, 2013.

———. "Official Bilateral Commitments by Sector." 2018. https://doi.org/10
.1787/data-00073-en.

Oelberger, Carrie R. "The Dark Side of Deeply Meaningful Work: Work-
Relationship Turmoil and the Moderating Role of Occupational Value
Homophily." *Journal of Management Studies* 56, no. 3 (2019): 558–88.
https://doi.org/10.1111/joms.12411.

Offutt, Stephen. *New Centers of Global Evangelicalism in Latin America and
Africa.* New York: Cambridge University Press, 2015.

Orsi, Robert A. *Thank You, St. Jude: Women's Devotion to the Patron Saint of Hopeless Causes*. New Haven, CT: Yale University Press, 1996.

Pattillo-McCoy, Mary. "Church Culture as a Strategy of Action in the Black Community." *American Sociological Review* 63, no. 6 (December 1998): 767. https://doi.org/10.2307/2657500.

Pew Research Center. *Global Attitudes and Trends, 2011–2013*. Accessed April 10, 2019. https://www.pewresearch.org/global/.

Plewes, Betty, and Rieky Stuart. "Opportunities and Challenges for International Volunteer Co-Operation." Montreal, Canada, 2007. http://forum-ids .org/wp-content/uploads/2012/07/Forum-2007-Future-Trends.pdf.

Polman, Linda. *The Crisis Caravan: What's Wrong with Humanitarian Aid*. New York: Picador, 2010.

Portes, Alejandro, and Lori D. Smith. *Institutions Count*. Berkeley: University of California Press, 2012.

Powell, Walter W., Aaron Horvath, and Christof Brandtner. "Click and Mortar: Organizations on the Web." *Research in Organizational Behavior* 36 (2016): 101–120.

Probasco, LiErin. "Giving Time, Not Money: Long-Term Impacts of Short-Term Mission Trips." *Missiology: An International Review* 41, no. 2 (April 2013): 202–24. https://doi.org/10.1177/0091829612 475166.

Putnam, Robert D. *Bowling Alone: The Collapse and Revival of American Community*. New York: Simon & Schuster, 2001.

Putnam, Robert D., and David E. Campbell. *American Grace: How Religion Divides and Unites Us*. New York: Simon & Schuster, 2010.

Queenan, Jeri Eckhard, Jacob Allen, and Jari Tuomala. "Stop Starving Scale: Unlocking the Potential of Global NGOs." *The Bridgespan Group*, April 2013. https://www.bridgespan.org/bridgespan/images/articles /stop-starving-scale-unlocking-the-potential/Stop-Starving-Scale .pdf?ext=.pdf.

Rodrik, Dani. "Goodbye Washington Consensus, Hello Washington Confusion? A Review of the World Bank's Economic Growth in the 1990s: Learning from a Decade of Reform." *Journal of Economic Literature* 44, no. 4 (2006): 973–87.

Rose-Ackerman, Susan. "Altruism, Nonprofits and Economic Theory." *Journal of Economic Literature* 34, no. 2 (June 1996): 701–28.

Rozario, Kevin. "'Delicious Horrors': Mass Culture, the Red Cross, and the Appeal of Modern American Humanitarianism."*American Quarterly* 55, no. 3 (2003): 417–55.

Rubenstein, Jennifer C. 2015. *Between Samaritans and States: The Political Ethics of Humanitarian INGOs.* Oxford: Oxford University Press.

Salamon, Lester M. "Of Market Failure, Voluntary Failure, and Third-Party Government: Toward a Theory of Government-Nonprofit Relations in the Modern Welfare State." *Journal of Voluntary Action Research* 16, nos. 1–2 (1987): 29–49.

Salamon, Lester M., S. Wojciech Sokolowski, and Megan Haddock. *Explaining Civil Society Development : A Social Origins Approach.* Baltimore: Johns Hopkins University Press, 2017.

Saxton, Gregory D., and Chao Guo. "Conceptualizing Web-Based Stake-holder Communication: The Organizational Website as a Stakeholder Relations Tool." *Communication & Science Journal*, 18 (2012).

Schmitz, Hans-Peter, Michael Dedmon, Tosca Bruno-van Vijfeijken, and Jaclyn Petruzzelli. "Democratizing Advocacy? NGOs, Digital Tools, and Organizational Repertoires." Working paper, 2019.

Schnable, Allison. "Religion and Giving for International Aid: Evidence from a Survey of U.S. Church Members." *Sociology of Religion* 76, no. 1 (2015a): 72–94. https://doi.org/10.1093/socrel/sru037.

———. "New American Relief and Development Organizations: Voluntarizing Global Aid." *Social Problems* 62, no. 2 (2015b): 309–29. https://doi.org/10 .1093/socpro/spv005 https://doi.org/10.1093/socpro/spv005.

———. "What Religion Affords Grassroots NGOs: Frames, Networks, Modes of Action." *Journal for the Scientific Study of Religion* 55, no. 2 (2016): 216–32.

Schnable, Allison, Anthony DeMattee, Rachel S. Robinson, and Jennifer N. Brass. "International Development Buzzwords: Understanding Their Use among Donors, NGOs, and Academics." *The Journal of Development Studies* (2020). https://doi.org/10.1080 /00220388.2020.1790532.

Sen, Amartya. *Development as Freedom.* New York: Knopf, 1999.

Shorette, Kristen. "Nongovernmental Regulation and Construction of Value in Global Markets: The Rise of Fair Trade, 1961–2006." *Sociological Perspectives* 57, no. 4 (2014): 526–47.

Simon, Bryant. "Not Going to Starbucks: Boycotts and the Out-Scouring of Politics in the Branded World." *Journal of Consumer Culture* 11, no. 2 (2011): 145–67.

Skocpol, Theda. *Diminished Democracy: From Membership to Management in American Civic Life*. Norman: University of Oklahoma Press, 2003.

Small, Mario Luis, David J. Harding, and Michèle Lamont. "Reconsidering Culture and Poverty." *The ANNALS of the American Academy of Political and Social Science* 629, no. 1 (May 2010): 6–27. https://doi.org/10.1177/0002716210362077.

Smilde, David. *Reason to Believe: Cultural Agency in Latin American Evangelicalism*. Berkeley: University of California Press, 2007.

Smith, Brian H. *More Than Altruism: The Politics of Private Foreign Aid*. Princeton, NJ: Princeton University Press, 1990.

———. "Nonprofit Organizations in International Development: Agents of Empowerment or Preservers of Stability?" In *Private Action and the Public Good*, edited by W. W. Powell and Elisabeth Clemens. New Haven, CT: Yale University Press, 1998.

Smith, Steven Rathgeb, and Michael Lipsky. *Nonprofits for Hire: The Welfare State in the Age of Contracting*. Cambridge, MA: Harvard University Press, 1993.

Snow, David A., and Robert D. Benford. "Ideology, Frame Resonance, and Participant Mobilization." *International Social Movement Research* 11, no. 1 (1988): 197–218.

———. "Master Frames and Cycles of Protest." In *Frontiers in Social Movement Theory*, edited by Aldon D. Morris and Carol McClurg Mueller, 133–55. New Haven, CT: Yale University Press, 1992.

Suárez, David F. "Collaboration and Professionalization: The Contours of Public Sector Funding for Nonprofit Organizations." *Journal of Public Administration Research and Theory* 21, no. 2 (2010): 307–26.

Swidler, Ann. "Culture in Action: Symbols and Strategies." *American Sociological Review* 51, no. 2 (April 1986): 273. https://doi.org/10.2307/2095521.

———. *Talk of Love: How Culture Matters*. Chicago: University of Chicago Press, 2001.

———. "Dialectics of Patronage: Logics of Accountability at the African AIDS-NGO Interface." In *Globalization, Philanthropy, and Civil Society: Projecting Institutional Logics Abroad*, edited by David C. Hammack and Steven Heydemann. Bloomington: Indiana University Press, 2009.

Swidler, Ann, and Susan Cotts Watkins. "'Teach a Man to Fish': The Sustainability Doctrine and Its Social Consequences." *World Development* 37, no. 7 (July 2009): 1182–96. https://doi.org/10.1016/j.worlddev.2008.11.002.

———. *A Fraught Embrace: The Romance and Reality of AIDS Altruism in Africa.* Princeton, NJ: Princeton University Press, 2017.

UNICEF South Asia. "Volunteering in Orphanages." Accessed August 7, 2019. https://www.unicef.org/rosa/what-we-do/child-protection/volunteering-orphanages.

US Agency for International Development. "Foreign Aid Explorer: The Official Record of U.S. Foreign Aid." Accessed January 24, 2019. https://explorer.usaid.gov/.

———. "Top 40 Vendors." Last modified May 7, 2019. https://www.usaid.gov/results-and-data/budget-spending/top-40-vendors

US Census Bureau; American Community Survey. "2013–2017 American Community Survey 5-Year Estimates: Selected Characteristics of the Foreign-Born Population by Region of Birth (Africa, Northern America, and Oceania), Table SO504." Accessed August 5, 2020. https://data.census.gov/cedsci/

———. "2013–2017 American Community Survey 5-Year Estimates: Selected Characteristics of the Foreign-Born Population by Region of Birth (Asia), Table SO505" U.S. Census Bureau. Accessed August 5, 2020. https://data.census.gov/cedsci/

———. "2013–2017 American Community Survey 5-Year Estimates: Selected Characteristics of the Foreign-Born Population by Region of Birth (Europe), Table SO503." Accessed August 5, 2020. https://data.census.gov/cedsci/

———. "2013–2017 American Community Survey 5-Year Estimates: Selected Characteristics of the Foreign-Born Population by Region of Birth (Latin America), Table SO506." Accessed August 5, 2020. https://data.census.gov/cedsci/

US Travel and Tourism Statistics. "US Citizen Traffic to Overseas Regions, Canada and Mexico 2015." National Tourism and Travel Office, 2015. https://travel.trade.gov/view/m-2015-O-001/index.html.

Vaisey, Stephen. "Motivation and Justification: A Dual-Process Model of Culture in Action." *American Journal of Sociology* 114, no. 6 (May 2009): 1675–1715. https://doi.org/10.1086/597179.

Ver Beek, Kurt Alan. "The Impact of Short-Term Missions: A Case Study of House Construction in Honduras after Hurricane Mitch." *Missiology: An International Review* 34, no. 4 (October 2006): 477–95. https://doi.org/10 .1177/009182960603400406.

Watkins, Susan Cotts, Ann Swidler, and Thomas Hannan. "Outsourcing Social Transformation: Development NGOs as Organizations." *Annual Review of Sociology* 38, no. 1 (August 11, 2012): 285–315. https://doi.org/10 .1146/annurev-soc-071811-145516.

Western Union. "2017 Annual Report." Englewood, CO: Western Union, 2017. http://s21.q4cdn.com/100551446/files/doc_financials/2017/AR /2018-proxy-statement.pdf.

White, Sarah. "Depoliticizing Development: The Uses and Abuses of Participation." In *The Participation Reader*, edited by A. Cornwall, 57–69. London: Zed Books, 2011.

"World Development: Aims and Scope." *World Development* 19, no. 6 (1991): 386.

Worthington, Samuel. "The Role of U.S. NGOs in Global Development and Humanitarian Work." Washington, DC: Interaction, 2013. http://www .interaction.org/files/FABB%202013_Sec01_PolicyPaper_RoleOfNGOs .pdf.

Wuthnow, Robert. *Acts of Compassion: Caring for Others and Helping Ourselves.* Princeton, NJ: Princeton University Press, 1991.

———. *Poor Richard's Principle: Recovering the American Dream through the Moral Dimension of Work, Business, and Money.* Princeton, N.J: Princeton University Press, 1996.

———. *Boundless Faith: The Global Outreach of American Churches.* Berkeley: University of California Press, 2009.

Wuthnow, Robert, and Stephen Offutt. "Transnational Religious Connections." *Sociology of Religion* 69, no. 2 (June 1, 2008): 209–32. https://doi .org/10.1093/socrel/69.2.209.

Index

American College of Emergency
Physicians, 39
American Friends Service
Committee, 9
Asia, 5–6, 9, 55, 83, 181, 190; INGOs
in, 50; progressive transformation
of development strategies in, 80;
and tourism, 12

Ben, 44–45
Black Lives Matter, 11
Blue Marble Dreams, 1–2, 4, 13, 127,
130; annual budget of, 2–3
Bosnia, 5, 85
brokers: dependence of INGOs on,
138–39; brokerage relationships in
the case study organizations,
131–39; as elites, 129; primary roles
of in grassroots INGOs, 130;
relationships with and downward
accountability, 127–31
Burundi, 55

Café Feminino, 58, 103–4
Campbell, David Todd, 161
capacity building, 56–59, 81, 88, 105,
111, 182, 190, 201, 217n3
CARE, 3, 8, 63, 65
Catholic Relief Services, 5, 9
Central America, 12
charity, 2, 7, 11–12, , 77–78, 122,
149, 176–178, 191, 211n2;
personal, 14–18, 25; public
(organization), 118, 194; religious,
160, 167–168
children, 13, 63–64, 92, 99, 102,
109–112, 134–136, 148–150, 164,
168, 180, 203–4; American, roles

for, 67, 150–52; images of, 6, 69,
144–45, 203; relationships
between parents and, 3, 13, 43, 55,
122, 184; sponsorship of, 22, 37–38,
61–62, 89, 124–25, 135, 153, 201;
street, 32–33; as students, 31, 111,
150, 169; as targeted recipients of
aid, 35, 48–49, 58, 68–72, 74,
96–97, 99–102, 128–29, 181, 189
China, 55, 82
Chitungwiza, 54
Christianity, globalized, 173
Church of Jesus Christ of Latter-day
Saints (LDS), 106
Church World Service, 8
Circle of Hope, 64, 171
citizen aid, 213n30
civil society, as a path to democratization and development, 6
Clara, 165, 172
climate change, 26, 145, 191
Cold War, the, 12
colonialism, 30, 53–54, 166, 200
Columbia University School of
International and Public
Affairs, 82
connective action, 11
consumerism, political, 11, 212n27
consumers, 12
culture, 7, 17, 57, 105, 113, 128–29, 132,
141, 145, 174–75, 181, 202;
exchange of, 57, 105, 113, 182, 195,
202, theories of, 159, 161, 166,
212n14, 220n7, 213n36
Czech Republic, 106

David, 34–35, 133–34
Deaton, Angus, 76–78

demand-driven explanations of the nonprofit sector. *See* nonprofit organizations, demand-driven and supply-driven explanations of

democracy, as a goal of development, 6–7, 77, 79; building of, 57, 59, 105, 202; engagement with, 118; institutions as a condition for development, 77

development, international, 113; international connections as the groundwork for establishing grassroots international NGOs, 83; as a personal process, 108–13, 183; professionalization of, 83; relationship between personal empowerment and, 110–11; volunteer-driven development, 213n30. *See also* development, international, transformation of the definition and the role of NGOs

development, international, transformation of the definition and the role of NGOs, 78–83; day-to-day roles of NGOs and transformation, 79–80; first-generation approaches to (relief and welfare), 80; second-generation approach to (community development), 80; shift in the role of NGOs, 81–82; third-generation approach to (sustainable systems), 80–81

discourse, borrowed from non-development domains, 16; on aid rationales, 71, 100; on aid

recipients, 70, 99; constraining effects of, 24, 219n3; of transformation, 101; webpages as sites for, 48–49

Dominican Republic, 110

donors, accountability to, 117–120, 127, 140; agencies, 79; and agency regulations, 9, 127, 177, 212n20; businesses, 65t8, 122, 202; donor fatigue, 126; individual, preferences of, 128, 132, 190; individual, as primary sources of funding for grassroots INGOs, 32, 49, 95, 123–27, 160, 180, 183; known to leaders of grassroots INGOS, 49, 123; perceptions by, 143–46, 150; preferences of, 6, 50, 60, 84, 120, 188; religious congregations as sources of, 158, 162–63, similarity with aid recipients, 102, 113; testimonials of, 61

Doris Duke Foundation, 41

Dryzek, John, 143–44

Dutch Private Development Initiatives, 215n1

Eco-Africa Papercraft, 54

Ecuador, cheese-making enterprise in, 110–11, 218n8

education, as development priority, 6, 77; of grassroots INGO supporters, 22, 30, 55–56, 91, 147, 177; medical, 17, 39–41, 89, 114; projects, 24, 31, 56, 57t5, 60, 60t6, 99, 101–4, 138–39, 141, 150–51, 167, 169, 171, 182, 189, 197, 202; as route to success, 16, 72, 91, 102–3, 110, 219n20

relationships with the United States in, 106; and contracting relationships with donors, 212n20; representations of suffering in, 145; rethinking of among Americans, 155–56

Good Works Global, 40

government, grassroots INGOs' discourse about, 107, 112, 114, 142; in aid-receiving countries, as foreign aid recipients, 5–6; in aid-receiving countries, collaboration with by grassroots INGOs, 17, 21, 31, 39, 41, 44, 65–66, 77, 111, 114, 118–19, 130, 140, 160, 163, 174, 182–83, 187, 190–91, 197; NGO registration with, 194; U.S., relationships with grassroots INGOs, 65tab., 65–68, 119, 163, 197; U.S., as aid donor, 5, 9, 53fig, 60, 60t, 65, 75, 161, 181; U.S., policies of, 145, 191. *See also* donors, agencies; foreign aid; Internal Revenue Service; official development assistance; US Agency for International Development

grassroots international nongovernmental organizations (INGOs), 4, 11, 13, 15, 155–56, 177–78, 191; accessing INGOs, 184–91; accountability of, 117–20; budgets of, 220–21n5; data concerning, 19–22, 47–48; deliberate avoidance of government by, 111–13; differences between INGOs and mainstream NGOs, 146–47; and donor perceptions, 146; education

as central to, 56–57; food/feeding programs of, 58–59; founding narratives of, 55–56; fundamental task of, 159–60; fundraising of, 122–23, 141–42; importance of individuals to, 182–83; medium-range analysis of, 20; personal aspects of (personal networks and relationships), 16–18, 127–31, 156, 180–81; popularity of medical projects among, 57–58; and the power of discourse, 143–47, 154–56; prevalence of Christian/Catholic ministry activities among, 59, 72–73; rationales for aid, 71–73, 72tab., 74, 96; registrations of with the IRS, 87–88; and the remaking of development aid, 17; and the shift from the "megarhetoric of development" to the micronarratives of development, 17–18; and short-term volunteers, 27–28; as supply-driven organizations, 184–85, 187–88; terminology used in describing, 193–95; and the understanding of development, 179–80; and US tax law, 59, 222n11; vision of development in as a personal process, 108–13; volunteers as leaders of, 180; websites of, 73–74, 111, 154, 158, 167, 195–97. *See also* amateurs, and grassroots international nongovernmental organizations (INGOs); grassroots international nongovernmental organizations (INGOs), and faith-based organizations;

US Agency for International Development (USAID), 9, 50, 56, 59–60, 95
USDA Organic, 11

Vicki, 91
volunteers/volunteering: emotional and spiritual experience of, 85–86, 112–13, 173–74, 186–87, 218n10; frustrations of, 125–26; generosity of, 109; motives of, 215n5; part-time volunteers as leaders of INGOs, 180; professional volunteers, 214n40; reliance of on personal networks to recruit volunteers, 124–25; short-term volunteers, 164–65; solicitation of volunteers with specialized skills, 87; volunteer–driven development, 213n30

Wallace Toronto Foundation, 106
WASH (water, sanitation, and hygiene). *See* sanitation, water
water, as development priority, 6, 73, 79; in religious framing, 167–168; projects by grassroots INGOs, 33, 57*tab.*, 58, 60, 68, 74, 98–99, 167, 182–83, 189, 191, 197, 201
Watkins, Susan Cotts, 78–79, 86, 110, 128; on "interstitial elites," 129

Wellsprings of Hope, 29*tab.*, 35–38, 56, 91, 125, 129; administration of by pastors, 158–59; Africa seen through the lens of, 151–54; brokerage relationships of, 134–35, 137–38; expansion of the programs offered by, 88–89; financial crisis of, 116–17; funding for, 123–24, 126, 152; reliance of on personal relationships, 86–87, 117
WINFOCUS, 40
women, as targeted aid recipients, 48, 69*tab.*, 69, 71, 74, 97*tab.*, 99, 101, 128, 169, 181–82, 197–198, 204; caring for children, 42, 110; effects of water shortages on, 168; empowerment of, 110; health of, 202; images of, 69, 145, 203; involved in income-generating projects, 34–35, 42–43, 54, 103–4, 110, 126; networks of, 54, 212n27; as small businesspersons, 1, 29*tab.*, 43, 58, 74, 90–91 101, 195, 212n8
Women Work Together, 54
World Bank, 56, 95, 120, 160
World Faiths Development Dialogue, 160
World Society theory, 212n14
World Vision, 3, 8; "partnership" originated by, 125

Founded in 1893,
UNIVERSITY OF CALIFORNIA PRESS
publishes bold, progressive books and journals
on topics in the arts, humanities, social sciences,
and natural sciences—with a focus on social
justice issues—that inspire thought and action
among readers worldwide.

The UC PRESS FOUNDATION
raises funds to uphold the press's vital role
as an independent, nonprofit publisher, and
receives philanthropic support from a wide
range of individuals and institutions—and from
committed readers like you. To learn more, visit
ucpress.edu/supportus.